A MANDATE TO EDUCATE

The Law and
Handicapped Children

Maggie Hume

An Education
Research Group
Report

Capitol Publications, Inc.
1101 King Street
Alexandria, Virginia 22314

Also published by the Education Research Group:

From Birth To Five: Serving The Youngest Handicapped Children
The Child Abuse Crisis: Impact on the Schools
P.L. 94-142: Impact on the Schools
AIDS: Impact on the Schools
Teen Pregnancy: Impact on the Schools
*Education Directory: A Guide to Decisionmakers in the Federal
    Government, the States and Education Associations*
Education Regulations Library
*The Education Evaluator's Workbook:
    How to Assess Education Programs*
*. . . And Education for All:
    Public Policy and Handicapped Children*

Copyright © 1987 by the Education Research Group,
    Capitol Publications, Inc.

Helen Hoart, Publisher
Roberta Weiner, Executive Editor

All rights reserved. No part of this book may be reproduced or used in any form without permission in writing from the publisher. Address inquiries to: Education Research Group, Capitol Publications, Inc., 1101 King St., Alexandria, Va. 22314, (703) 683-4100.

Printed in the United States of America

Library of Congress Catalog Card Number 87-70906
ISBN 0-937925-27-6

Maggie Hume
    A Mandate to Educate: The Law and Handicapped Children

Cover design by Linda C. McDonald

First Edition

KF
4210
.H86
1987

Table Of Contents

	Page
Introduction	5

Part One:

Litigation History	9
Legal Milestones	15

Part Two:

The Future Of Special Education Litigation	21
A Free, Appropriate Public Education	23
Placement In The Least Restrictive Environment	28
AIDS	30
Related Services	32
The 1986 EHA Amendments	36
The Medicaid Conflict	37
The Supreme Court Takes Up Discipline	39
Due Process	43
Mediation	45
Attorneys' Fees	46
The Shortcomings Of Litigation	50

Appendix

Text Of The Education Of The Handicapped Act	55

About The Author

Maggie Hume is editor of *Education of the Handicapped*, a biweekly Capitol Publications newsletter on public policy and handicapped children, and a reporter for *Education Daily*. Ms. Hume previously edited *School Law News,* a sister newsletter on developments in school law. She is the author of *The Supreme Court and Education: The 1985-86 Term* and was a contributing writer to *AIDS: Impact on the Schools*. Prior to joining Capitol, Ms. Hume worked for Fairchild Publications in New York and Washington, D.C. She has a bachelor of arts degree in literature from Yale University.

Introduction

Schools have a mandate to educate all handicapped children. But what exactly does that mean?
- What defines a handicapped child under the Education for All Handicapped Children Act, P.L. 94-142?
- What is the definition of education? And how do you decide what related services you are legally required to provide each handicapped child to help him or her benefit from an education?
- When is integration appropriate and when is the least restrictive environment for a severely handicapped child actually a segregated setting?

The questions began when P.L. 94-142 was enacted in 1975 and have shown no signs of easing up in the 12 years that have passed since then. Indeed, the volume of questions has increased dramatically since the enactment of the 1986 Education of the Handicapped Amendments, P.L. 99-457, which set up two new programs for handicapped infants, toddlers and preschoolers.

This book is an attempt to synthesize the history of special education litigation—both before the P.L. 94-142's passage and since—with the future of litigation as noted attorneys in the field predict it.

* * *

Thanks are due to Nancy Jones of the Congressional Research Service for reviewing the manuscript and offering helpful suggestions and Laurie Evans for her careful copyediting. Thanks also go to Roberta Weiner, executive editor of the Education Research Group, for guidance and encouragement.

Acknowledgements also are due to Leslie A. Ratzlaff, managing editor of the Education Research Group, who coordinated production of the book, Linda C. McDonald, who designed the cover, and Cynthia Peters, who did the typesetting.

Maggie Hume

Part One
Litigation History

Litigation History

> *"In these days, it is doubtful that any child may reasonably be expected to succeed in life if he is denied the opportunity of an education. Such an opportunity . . . is a right which must be made available to all on equal terms."*
> — U.S. Supreme Court,
> Brown v. Board of Education, 1954

Two decades before Congress enacted P.L. 94-142, the U.S. Supreme Court cleared a path for special education law, in a case in which the students who sued were not handicapped: the racial desegregation decision in *Brown v. Board of Education* (347 U.S. 483).

"In these days," wrote the justices, in a passage quoted by congressional authors of P.L. 94-142, "it is doubtful that any child may reasonably be expected to succeed in life if he is denied the opportunity of an education. Such an opportunity, where the state has undertaken to provide it, is a right which must be made available to all on equal terms."

In the late 1960s, handicapped rights advocates brought the principle of *Brown*—the bold application of the Constitution's equal protection clause—to their own clients' cases. Results at first were mixed or limited.

Then lightning struck in 1971 with *Pennsylvania Association of Retarded Citizens (PARC) v. Commonwealth* (334 F. Supp. 1257). In a consent decree that settled a class action for mentally retarded children, Pennsylvania discarded a state law that relieved schools of the responsibility to enroll "uneducable" or "untrainable" children. On the basis of extensive expert testimony, the federal district court in Philadelphia entered a "finding" that mentally retarded children can benefit from education and are entitled to it.

"The groundbreaking lightning bolt there was [the notion] that these kids could learn. Up until then we warehoused our kids in institutions, because 'those poor kids aren't educable, God bless them,'" remembered Reed Martin, an attorney with Advocacy Inc.

in Texas. "*PARC* was a consciousness-raising; it wasn't just a legal decision. It printed the bumper stickers" for disability rights.

But *PARC* may have gone further than the case warranted, some school lawyers say. "I think we could have come to where we are without *PARC*," said Gwen Gregory, deputy general counsel at the National School Boards Association (NSBA). "We may have come a lot further [by litigation] than we had to come."

Just one year after *PARC*, the federal district court in Washington, D.C., went further in *Mills v. Board of Education* (348 F. Supp. 866). While admitting it was not living up to its duty to provide special education for handicapped children, the city school board pleaded lack of funds as an excuse. But the court quoted *Brown*'s "equal terms" language and said the board had to educate all pupils, whatever their handicaps, even if funds were tight. Constitutional rights are rights even if they are costly, the court said, ruling that handicapped students should no more bear the brunt of the district's financial or administrative shortcomings than nonhandicapped students do.

The *PARC* agreement and the *Mills* ruling laid not just the foundation but some of the building blocks of P.L. 94-142. Not only did handicapped children win access to school, but the state had to locate and evaluate them and design for each an individual program. Schools could not change placements without due process, and integration was favored over more restrictive placements.

The two cases later were credited with establishing the right of handicapped children to special public education, but still, "there wasn't a clear precedent" that could be transferred to every state beyond Pennsylvania and the District of Columbia, said Martin. "So when you took a case between '71 and '75, you knew you could win; you just had to be creative." Between *Mills* and the passage of P.L. 94-142, special education advocates pursued at least 46 suits in 28 states.

Courts at first were loath to involve themselves in the day-to-day operations of schools, their hands already full with desegregation, busing and equal education for women. In that atmosphere, some school districts thought they had nothing to fear, according to Martin, while others were struggling to figure out exactly what was required of them and how they were expected to pay for it.

Congress passed P.L. 94-142 in 1975, and "From '77 to '80, there was this very heady time when you could win any case," if you represented the handicapped child, said Martin. "It was like shooting fish in a barrel."

As schools adjusted to the act, the pace of litigation steadied. Meanwhile, implementation of the rulings handicapped students won was sometimes slow: eight years after *Mills,* the Washington, D.C., school board was held in contempt of court for failing to meet the timetables set out in the decision.

Once handicapped students had access to school, by and large, litigation turned to the questions that arose there and the definitions of terms under P.L. 94-142: discipline, payment for private placements, racially discriminatory testing, related services, extended services, the definition of "appropriate" education and other issues.

The year P.L. 94-142 became law, the U.S. Supreme Court spoke on students' rights during disciplinary action in *Goss v. Lopez* (419 U.S. 565), which was the basis for later discipline rulings concerning handicapped students. Calling the right to a public education a protected property interest, which cannot be revoked without due process, *Goss* overturned an Ohio law allowing suspensions of up to 10 days with no hearing.

For any suspension, a student has the right to "notice of the charges against him" and some hearing, "at least an informal give-and-take between student and disciplinarian, preferably prior to the suspension," the Court said. Suspensions longer than 10 days or expulsions "may require more formal procedures;" on the other hand, "in unusual situations," even a short suspension may require "something more than the rudimentary procedures."

Special education raised special questions, answered in disparate rulings that culminated finally in two federal appeals court decisions. In 1981, the 5th U.S. Circuit Court of Appeals ruled in *S-1 v. Turlington* (635 F.2d 342; cert. denied, 454 U.S. 1030) that expulsion is a change of placement demanding a hearing and due process consistent with P.L. 94-142, provided the misbehavior is a manifestation of the handicap. Also, the child must continue receiving some services after an expulsion, *S-1* said.

The court also assigned to the school the burden of determining whether the misconduct is a manifestation of the student's handicap. School officials often are not qualified to determine whether misbehavior is caused by the child's handicap, and a specialist may have to make that judgment, the court added. The 6th Circuit reached the same conclusion the next year in *Kaelin v. Grubbs* (682 F.2d 595).

Meanwhile, Pennsylvania, home of the landmark *PARC* case, became the scene of another groundbreaking ruling, when the 3rd Circuit in 1980 affirmed a decision in *Battle v. Commonwealth of Pennsylvania* (629 F.2d 269) that overturned a state policy against offering summer school. The court said a 180-day limit on the public school schedule violated P.L. 94-142 because it precluded proper determination of what constitutes an appropriate education.

NSBA predicted an $830 million jump in the yearly cost of special education, nationwide, after *Battle*. Despite the association's pleas, the Supreme Court let the ruling stand (452 U.S. 968). Court after court came to the same decision, requiring extended programming where it would benefit a child. The principle disturbed the schools. "I think the potential was there for tremendous problems," Gregory said, "but I don't think that has happened."

The Supreme Court did not take a case under P.L. 94-142 until 1981, when it heard *Hendrick Hudson v. Rowley* (458 U.S. 176), in which parents sued the school system to obtain a sign-language interpreter for their deaf daughter. Amy Rowley was well-adjusted and performing above average in her first grade class, and the school had gone to considerable lengths for her, but she would have been doing better if not for her handicap, noted the district court. The court said an appropriate education is one that provides "an opportunity to achieve [a child's] full potential commensurate with the opportunity provided to other children."

"The handicapped groups were not happy about that case going up, because the facts were so good for the school district," NSBA's Gregory said. "Really, it was almost a situation where you couldn't lose it."

In its 1982 ruling, the Court said P.L. 94-142 guarantees handicapped students an educational opportunity, but not an equal educational opportunity. The school is not required to "maximize each [handicapped] child's potential 'commensurate with the opportunity provided other children,'" the Court said, noting that schools cannot even equalize nonhandicapped students' chances of maximizing their potential.

The justices also told courts to limit themselves to two questions in special education cases. The first is whether the state has complied with the procedures in the act, including adopting—through the district—an individualized education program (IEP) conforming to the law. The second asks whether the IEP is "reasonably calculated to enable the child to receive educational benefits." For a child mainstreamed in a regular classroom, the IEP "should be reasonably calculated to enable the child to achieve passing marks and advance from grade to grade," the Court added.

Joe Scherer, associate executive director of the American Association of School Administrators at the time, was relieved. "We don't want to deny the opportunity [of] adequate education," he said then, "but we don't want to be providing the Cadillac of the line." For schools, the ruling meant the courts would defer more to their educational judgment.

Handicapped rights advocates initially were unsettled by the

Litigation History

limits imposed by *Rowley*. Finally, however, "everybody claimed a win," Gregory said. The decision, after all, upheld the basic tenets of P.L. 94-142. Things could have gone a lot worse for handicapped children, advocacy groups said.

The Supreme Court two years later in *Irving Independent School District v. Tatro* (468 U.S. 883) said Amber Tatro was entitled to catheterization at school. Tatro, who could catheterize herself by the time her case reached the high court, had the service performed by a school nurse every three to four hours because delaying it could cause kidney damage.

The school district argued, "Catheterization today, kidney dialysis tomorrow." But the unanimous Court quoted P.L. 94-142's definition of free appropriate education as "special education and [such] related services . . . as may be required to assist a handicapped child to benefit from special education." Catheterization for Tatro amounted to access to school; without it, her IEP would not conform to the act.

The district pointed out that the act excludes medical services other than diagnostics, but the Court responded that catheterization does not require a licensed physician, the crucial factor established in the Education Department regulations. In fact, a layperson with less than an hour's training could do the job in a few minutes.

Later that year, the Supreme Court without comment refused to review a 3rd Circuit decision in *Piscataway Township Board of Education v. T.G.* (cert. denied, 53 U.S.L.W. 3436) that said psychotherapy for an emotionally disturbed student qualifies as a related service under P.L. 94-142. *Piscataway* is one of a line of cases that distinguish psychological services by a licensed physician—not provided under the act—from those of a psychologist, who is not a medical doctor.

The lower courts meanwhile continued working out the special education response to generic education questions. In *Debra P. v. Turlington* (644 F.2d 397 and 730 F.2d 1405), the 5th and 11th circuits found Florida's minimum competency test—a prerequisite for graduation—racially discriminatory because black students failed in disproportionate numbers as a result of prior segregation. The courts also said a state must give students timely notice of the requirement (probably upon entering high school), establish the validity of its test and guarantee that the material on it was presented in the curriculum.

As *Goss* did in the discipline area, *Debra P.* laid the groundwork for judicial standards on graduation requirements for special education students. In 1983, the 7th Circuit upheld the right of a school district to require handicapped students to pass examinations before receiving diplomas, in *Brookhart v. Illinois State Board of Education* (697 F.2d 179). And in 1984 the Supreme Court refused to review a New York school board's challenge of the use of competency tests as a graduation requirement for handicapped children, in *Board of Education v. Ambach* (458 N.Y.S., 2d 680, 684 [N.Y. App. Div. 1982]). The state has since created special education diplomas for students completing their IEPs.

While the lower courts enforced the school district's responsibility for the costs of private placement under an IEP, the Supreme Court went further in 1985, in a ruling that surprised even some special education advocacy workers.

The Court decided unanimously, in *Burlington School Committee v. Department of Education* (53 U.S.L.W. 4509), that parents who unilaterally place their handicapped children in private schools are entitled to reimbursement if a court later finds the placement is more appropriate than what the public school had offered.

"I think a lot of the reason people were surprised [by *Burlington*] was that they had lived with the *Stemple* doctrine," Gregory said, referring to a 1980 ruling by the 4th Circuit, *Stemple v. Board of Education of Prince George's County* (623 F.2d 893). *Stemple* said parents who unilaterally transfer their child are not necessarily entitled to tuition reimbursement, and the Supreme Court declined to review the case.

Smith v. Robinson (468 U.S. 992), the Supreme Court's only other decision so far under P.L. 94-142, immediately was "appealed"—to Congress—and overruled. In *Smith* a divided Court held that P.L. 94-142 is the exclusive avenue for relief in special education complaints, and because the act, in all its detail, did not provide for attorneys' fees for parents who win their cases, parents cannot collect fees from schools by adding claims under Section 504 of the 1973 Rehabilitation Act or other federal civil rights laws.

The 1986 bill that overturned *Smith,* the Handicapped Children's Protection Act, P.L. 99-372, states it is Congress's intent that fees be allowed under P.L. 94-142. Under P.L. 99-372, once parents have exhausted all administrative routes to resolving a special education dispute, they may sue a district not only under P.L. 94-142 but under the Rehabilitation Act, the Constitution and the statute allowing for suits that allege a deprivation of a federal right by a state or local agency.

But the issue is not ready to rest in peace. With the ink barely dry after the president signed the measure, school attorneys were questioning the law's retroactivity and its provision for fees for legal work in cases resolved at the administrative levels. Their questions are sure to have a day in court.

Meanwhile the Supreme Court announced its fifth foray into P.L. 94-142: The justices in early 1987 agreed to review the law's "stay put" provision as it applies to discipline of students whose handicap is responsible for violent misbehavior. In the lower court ruling, the 9th Circuit said that apart from imposing a limited disciplinary suspension, a school district cannot change a violent student's special education placement over parental objections without going through the normal due process steps to adopt a new education plan.

Although that case, *Honig v. Doe* (55 U.S.L.W. 3569), just reached the Supreme Court, and other cases certainly may follow, the federal courts in more than a decade of P.L. 94-142 litigation have issued guidance on many of the most important and commonly occurring issues.

"There's still going to be lots and lots of little, annual battles, but hopefully we've got some standards," said Martin. "What I worry about is, somewhere some kid is going to be getting catheterization, get an infection, get kidney damage, and sue the school."

P.L. 94-142: LEGAL MILESTONES IN THE EDUCATION OF HANDICAPPED CHILDREN

1954
Brown v. Board of Education of Topeka, 347 U.S. 483

The U.S. Supreme Court ruled that the opportunity of an education, where the state has undertaken to provide it, is a right that must be made available to all on equal terms.

1971
Pennsylvania Association for Retarded Children (PARC) v. Commonwealth of Pennsylvania, 334 F. Supp. 1257 (E.D. Pa. 1971) and 343 F. Supp. 279 (E.D. Pa. 1972)

Settling a class action suit for the right to education for retarded children, the court-approved consent decree stated that all mentally retarded persons are capable of benefiting from education, and they have a right to a public education. The case overturned a Pennsylvania statute relieving the state of responsibility to educate students classified as uneducable or untrainable.

1972
Mills v. Board of Education of the District of Columbia, 348 F. Supp. 866 (D.D.C. 1972)

The federal district court ordered that if the school system's funds are insufficient for all the programs that are needed and desirable, then the available funds must be spent equitably so that no child is entirely excluded from education consistent with his or her needs and ability to benefit. The financial or administrative inadequacies of the school system should not bear more heavily on handicapped children than on nonhandicapped children.

1975
Goss v. Lopez, 419 U.S. 565 (1975)

The U.S. Supreme Court ruled that students suspended for 10 days or fewer have the right to an informal conference, and that suspensions longer than 10 days may require a formal hearing. Though the students involved here were not handicapped, the decision became the basis of later discipline rulings in special education.

1975
Passage of P.L. 94-142

1980
Battle v. Commonwealth of Pennsylvania, 629 F.2d 269 (3rd Cir. 1980) [on appeal of the decision in *Armstrong v. Kline*, 476 F. Supp. 583 (E.D. P.A. 1979)]; cert. denied, 452 U.S. 968 (1981)

The circuit court overturned a Pennsylvania state policy against offering summer school, saying that a 180-day limit on instruction precludes proper determination of what constitutes an appropriate education under P.L. 94-142.

1981
S-1 v. Turlington, 635 F.2d 342 (5th Cir. 1981); cert. denied, 454 U.S. 1030 (1981)

The circuit court ruled that expelling a student for reasons related to his or her handicap is a change of placement, which requires a hearing consistent with P.L. 94-142 due process procedures; that services cannot cease completely even if a student is expelled; and that determining whether misbehavior is related to a student's handicap typically is not within the expertise of school board members. Followed by a similar circuit court decision, *Kaelin v. Grubbs*, 682 F.2d 595 (6th Cir. 1982).

Litigation History

1981 and 1984
Debra P. v. Turlington, 644 F.2d 397 (5th Cir. 1981) and 730 F.2d 1405 (11th Cir. 1984)

The circuit courts ruled that a state must establish the validity of its minimum competency tests and, if the tests are a prerequisite for graduation, ensure that the material on the tests was included in the curriculum. Though the *Debra P.* students were not handicapped, the decision became the basis of later special education rulings on testing.

Similar rulings applying those principles to special education, mainly on the basis of the Constitution's equal protection and due process clauses and Section 504 of the Rehabilitation Act, included *Anderson v. Banks*, 520 F. Supp. 472 (S.D. Ga. 1981), modified, 540 F. Supp. 761 (1982); *Northport-East Northport Union Free School District v. Ambach*, 458 N.Y.S.2d 680, 684 (N.Y. App. Div. 1982); and *Brookhart v. Illinois State Board of Education*, 697 F.2d 179 (7th Cir. 1983).

1982
Hendrick Hudson Central School District v. Rowley, 458 U.S. 176 (1982)

Reversing the district and appeals courts, the U.S. Supreme Court ruled 6-3 that federal law does not guarantee that handicapped students' individualized instruction will maximize their potential commensurate with the opportunities provided other children. The ruling strengthened earlier lower court decisions, such as *Bales v. Clarke*, 523 F. Supp. 1366, 1370 (E.D. Va. 1981), which said P.L. 94-142 does not require that the "best" program be selected, only that the selected program be appropriate.

1984
Irving Independent School District v. Tatro, 468 U.S. 883

The U.S. Supreme Court unanimously held that catheterization is a "related service" that schools must provide to students who need it during the school day, and the Court buttressed Education Department regulations defining "related services" to include school health services that don't have to be performed by a licensed physician.

1984
Smith v. Robinson, 468 U.S. 992

The U.S. Supreme Court ruled 6-3 that parents who win their cases under P.L. 94-142 cannot collect fees for their cases merely by adding claims under the 14th Amendment, Section 1983 of the 1971 Civil Rights Act or Section 504 of the 1973 Rehabilitation Act.

1985
Burlington School Committee v. Department of Education, 53 U.S.L.W. 4509

The U.S. Supreme Court ruled unanimously that parents who unilaterally place their handicapped children in private schools are entitled to receive tuition reimbursement if the placement is ultimately deemed proper in court.

1987
Honig v. Doe, 55 U.S.L.W. 3569

The Supreme Court agreed to review a 1986 decision by the 9th Circuit (called *Doe v. Maher* [793 F.2d 1470]) saying that — apart from a limited suspension set by state law — a school cannot change a violent student's special education placement without adopting a new education plan and giving the parents a chance to challenge it; courts may order exceptions in "truly exigent" cases, however. *Maher* also said the state education agency must serve an individual handicapped child directly if that pupil's school district has failed to provide a free, appropriate public education. The Court was likely to rule on both questions by July 1988.

Part Two
The Future Of Special Education Litigation

The Future Of Special Education Litigation

"Parents and guardians will not lack ardor in seeking to ensure that handicapped children receive all of the benefits to which they are entitled by the Act."
— U.S. Supreme Court,
Hendrick Hudson Central School District v. Rowley, 1982

The mandate to educate all handicapped children is simple: "It is the purpose of this Act to assure that all handicapped children have available to them . . . a free appropriate public education which emphasizes special education and related services designed to meet their unique needs," states the 1975 Education for All Handicapped Children Act, P.L. 94-142.

But implementing the mandate means defining what is appropriate, establishing the related services and ensuring that unique needs are met for 4.4 million children each year. The issues are so complicated and provoke such intense—sometimes bitter—emotions that P.L. 94-142 is known as one of Congress's more intricate and heavily litigated pieces of legislation.

While litigation through the first years under P.L. 94-142 focused on access to education and the appropriateness of education, it has since graduated to a second generation of issues. Many suits relating to only one child's placement or services have little transferability to other students.

In contrast to the early role of litigation in winning access to education, "I see litigation in the future less as a vehicle for solving problems . . . [and] more a tool for resolving policy," said Frederick Weintraub, assistant executive director of the Council for Exceptional Children (CEC). Educators agree special education is good policy; the chief problems now relate to lack of resources to implement the policy, Weintraub said. "I don't think advocacy lawyers—

though I don't think they would admit it — like 94-142; it doesn't provide room for class action suits."

But a number of advocacy lawyers maintain that important legal questions remain to be answered, and they do not rule out class action litigation. Arlene Mayerson, directing attorney for the Disability Rights Education & Defense Fund (DREDF), said more judicial guidance is needed on "appropriateness" and related services questions. As the state of the art of special education evolves, litigation also will confront new issues; yesterday's unimaginable related service may be feasible tomorrow.

Mayerson also insists litigation remains a needed and valid tool in securing full implementation of P.L. 94-142. Suits may focus, for example, on enforcement of a few areas of the act throughout a state or major school system, particularly the areas that received least attention during the law's first years. Advocacy groups say some of those areas are secondary and vocational education; placement and services for the most severely retarded and institutionalized children; due process; and services for incarcerated handicapped youth.

New issues have come up as well: services for children with acquired immune deficiency syndrome (AIDS); the award of attorneys' fees to parents who prevail in administrative due process hearings on their children's programs; 1986 amendments to the Education of the Handicapped Act (EHA), which extend services to infants and preschoolers and include new financial arrangements; and the U.S. Supreme Court's 1987 announcement that it will consider discipline in special education.

And in the trenches of administrative hearings and litigation, as one school lawyer says, "we continue to rehash the same issues" of placement and services. As regular education in the 1980s has emphasized "achieving excellence in education, . . . the question in special education is whether these kids can achieve that [and] whether there's going to be continuing commitment to giving these kids education," added Jane Stern, who until early 1987 was executive director of Advocates for Children in New York City.

"The question [during such litigation] is, what are the issues people are most likely to go to the wall for?" said Martin Gerry, Washington-based advocacy attorney who, from 1975 to 1977, led the Office for Civil Rights in the old Department of Health, Education and Welfare. "It's not necessarily the most important thing. It's often the one with the most money involved," such as residential placement or expensive related services, said Gerry, who is president of the Fund for Equal Access to Society.

A Free Appropriate Public Education

Many of the legal questions arising under P.L. 94-142 concern the core requirement that states offer each handicapped student an "appropriate" public education. The U.S. Supreme Court's 1982 ruling in *Hendrick Hudson Central School District v. Rowley* (458 U.S. 176) and federal appeals court rulings supply broad guidance on what constitutes appropriate education and what does not, but to some experts, the word "appropriate" always can use further clarification. Still others expect some currently accepted definitions of "appropriate" to be reconsidered and narrowed in light of *Rowley*.

In *Rowley*, the Court denied a bright and well-adjusted deaf student a sign language interpreter and said it is not a requirement of an appropriate education under P.L. 94-142 to "maximize each [handicapped] child's potential 'commensurate with the opportunity provided other children.'"

Districts must, however, obey any state standards that exceed the federal requirements, two federal appeals courts agreed in 1985: the 1st Circuit in *David D. v. Dartmouth School Committee* (775 F.2d 411; cert. denied, 54 U.S.L.W. 3716) and the 3rd Circuit in *Geis v. Board of Education of Parsippany-Troy Hills, Morris County, N.J.* (774 F.2d 575).

* * *

Year-round programming and extended school days have been among the most frequently raised "appropriate" education questions. In a trend-setting ruling in *Battle v. Pennsylvania* (629 F.2d 269), the 3rd Circuit in 1980 overturned a state policy against offering summer school. While summer services are not automatically required for handicapped students, the 3rd Circuit said a 180-day limit on the public school schedule violated P.L. 94-142 because it precluded proper determination of what constitutes an appropriate education.

That ruling came in 1980, but some parents and schools have continued clashing over extended services, according to Reed Martin, a leading handicap advocacy attorney. "The approach [courts have] taken up to now has been, 'you can't say automatically that you won't do more than 180 days,'" Martin said. But "that doesn't leave [schools] with a very workable standard for what a child needs" and what a school should provide, he said.

"So what we see is schools saying, 'Okay, for multihandicapped kids facing severe regression, we'll do two hours a day, five days a week for the month of June,'" Martin said. "That doesn't in any way address the need for summer services."

Martin attributed disputes over extended services to a tendency of schools and parents to write the student's individualized education program (IEP) with sketchy goals. "It's not unusual for an IEP to have a goal of 'mathematics' or a goal to 'improve motor performance.' That's it, no short-term objectives," he said. Parents and educators could avoid the disputes and litigation, Martin indicated, by "real concrete goal setting, saying 'Johnny is now at [step] 3 and we want to get him at 19. And if June comes and Johnny is only at 7, then we need summer programming.'"

Now, according to Advocacy Inc., where Martin practices in Austin, Texas, "Virtually every court to examine the issue of summer programming has struck down public school policies that deny summer services." Courts that have followed *Battle* in a spate of rulings include:

- the 11th Circuit in 1985 ruling in *Georgia Association of Retarded Citizens v. McDaniel* (716 F.2d 1565; cert. denied, 53 U.S.L.W. 3599);
- the 8th Circuit in 1986 in *Yaris v. Special School District of St. Louis County* (780 F.2d 724); and
- the 5th Circuit's *Alamo Heights Independent School District v. Texas Board of Education* (790 F.2d 1133) in 1986.

The same principle has been applied to the number of years a handicapped student stays in public school. The 10th Circuit in 1985's *Helms v. Independent School District No. 3* (750 F.2d 820; cert. denied, 105 S.Ct. 2024) said districts could not apply to handicapped students a state policy of never providing more than 12 years of public education.

The "court found that the graduation of handicapped students was a sham designed to terminate the school system's responsibility at the earliest possible moment," observed Nancy Jones, a legislative attorney for the Congressional Research Service (CRS).

P.L. 94-142 requires decisionmaking on the basis of individual students' needs, Advocacy Inc. emphasized in a 1986 briefing paper for parents. "Any policy that attempts to be categorical . . . breaks the law," according to the group.

* * *

But Jean Bilger Arnold, a Blacksburg, Va., attorney who represents school districts in special education cases, said courts should hone down the situations in which extended services are required. Arnold said the 1980 *Battle* decision, which required schools to consider year-round programming, may have been read too broadly at first. Fine-tuning is required, she said.

Some experts look at *Rowley* as a basis for that fine-tuning, saying the decision may encourage courts to think twice before requiring a school to offer year-round courses or longer school days to a special education student.

In a similar vein, Arnold saw a trend toward questioning the point of educational services for the most severely handicapped students or those some consider uneducable. The question has been "in the mind of educators since the passage of the act," she said. "Schools have been serving children even though the services are almost noneducational—students that are almost nonfunctional, where you may have a teacher going in and turning them over on a mat."

The problem may be that community health services have shifted quasi-medical, barely educational services to the schools. "But the educational question is, is there a point at which an individual is so handicapped that he can't benefit from education?" Arnold said. "There may be a tendency toward further action there—not a lot, but some—especially as federal and state budgets get tighter and tighter."

* * *

Another area that may become a subject for litigation on "appropriate" education is program quality, with advocacy lawyers arguing that poor programs, even if the hours are ample, are not "appropriate."

"An area where I think you're going to see a lot of action, and I'm trying to go out there and stir some up, is secondary programming," Gerry said. While the first years of P.L. 94-142 saw "an enormous pressure from both parents and school districts" to implement effective elementary education programs, secondary education lagged, Gerry said. Ironically, litigation grows more likely as more schools implement good programs of secondary education and transition to life after school, he added. "The more [good programs] there are, the less satisfied parents will be" if their children are left out.

Of those not receiving an adequate secondary education, some seem to drop from the IEP rolls, even though they may still need special education, while others move into residential institutions that may "warehouse" more than educate them, attorneys charged. Finally, a number of retarded or learning disabled children who remain in high schools with IEPs suffer through irrelevant programming, Gerry contended.

"Too many schools very simplistically reason, if they learned A through L in elementary school, they should learn M through Z in secondary school," he said. "But there's no way you're going to teach a real learning disabled kid M through Z, and no reason to since he wouldn't be using it. There's no point in trying to teach the alphabet to someone who's not verbal when he really needs to learn to cross the street."

Where secondary programming is insufficient, retarded and other handicapped children may receive no meaningful preparation for independent living, advocates say. "If you want your child to live in something other than an institution, and have a job perhaps, you have to develop skills," Gerry said.

"I think we'll see a new generation of cases on what kind of education poor, inner city, minority students are getting," he said. "Consigning kids to dead-end programs" by classifying them as mentally retarded on the basis of unsound intelligence exams, he said, is "rearing itself again as an issue."

Dropouts could be the subject of related litigation. "We see the dropout problem as an access issue," said New York's Stern. "If programs and services are not structured in a way to maintain [handicapped students in school], and there is poor attendance, they are denied access. A system that actually encourages kids to leave . . . goes beyond the latitude allowed in the *Rowley* case. That violates the spirit of the law."

* * *

Critics say the greatest gap in secondary programming usually is vocational education, which they have called "a very, very, very big problem," a "systemic" problem and "minimal or useless." Predicting that the first secondary education suits would erupt in that area, Gerry added, "I think the schools are far from ready for it."

Even CEC's Weintraub, who otherwise downplayed litigation, said vocational education could produce class action litigation against schools, districts or state education agencies. Since P.L. 94-142 was enacted, there has been "greater access to vocational education, but we don't have access to those parts of voc ed that are meaningful: apprentice programs and the other kinds of programs that lead to jobs," he said.

A consistent, widespread pattern of poor or sparse vocational education for handicapped students could make a state liable for a suit on the grounds it is not providing an appropriate education, said Paul Weckstein, director of the Center for Law and Education's (CLE) Washington, D.C., office.

The Future Of Special Education Litigation 27

"You may make the case that at least for every kid who is not going on to college it may be appropriate," Weckstein suggested, adding that only a small percentage of those students do receive vocational education. "It's not clear to me that [the law's provision for vocational education] has ever been adequately enforced," he said.

But P.L. 94-142 may not be the best vehicle for vocational education cases. More effective laws would be Section 504 of the 1973 Rehabilitation Act and the 1984 reauthorization of federal vocational programs (the Carl Perkins Vocational Education Act), civil rights lawyers said. Discrimination claims, rather than "appropriate education" claims, could be brought under those acts, Weckstein said.

"The handicapped have been denied access to the best programs and shunted to sheltered workshops," Weckstein charged. Section 504, which forbids discrimination on the basis of disability in federally funded activities, would apply because many schools receive federal grants under the Vocational Education Act: The Perkins Act ensures that each state will spend an amount equal to 20 percent of its federal vocational education grant on handicapped students, and it encourages schools to educate handicapped students alongside nonhandicapped students.

* * *

New York's Stern, who worked for years on enforcement of a ruling against New York City, named other areas where school districts have had great difficulty complying with the law. It is hard for multilingual districts—New York at least—to meet the "very stringent requirements in P.L. 94-142 for involving [non-English-speaking] parents in the full spectrum of due process rights," she said.

Stern also said enforcement action is needed to serve homeless children, a disproportionate number of whom will be eligible for special education, and undocumented aliens. The parents of those children, if they are available, cannot be expected to spend hours in "middle-class-oriented due process hearings," she said.

Another problem, touching fewer children, is that the surrogate parent provision of P.L. 94-142 is "just something that hasn't been implemented," said Kathleen Boundy, an attorney in CLE's Boston office. The act entitles any child without parental representation to a surrogate parent, but many times it is not clear who is responsible for filling the role.

The confusion is deepest in the cases of institutionalized children, she said. Who should the surrogate be? "Are we talking about the directors of these institutions? Or are the children wards of the state?"

The issue overlaps the problems incarcerated handicapped children may face, Boundy said. One difficulty is that the intended duration of their stay often is unclear. Also, many have had no testing and lack an IEP. "Incarcerated youth have a higher rate of disability, especially learning disability, and they're not being served," Boundy said. Even where there is an IEP, another lawyer said, it often is not implemented.

Placement In The Least Restrictive Environment

Because placement can be a very emotional and costly decision, the issue is likely to remain at the center of many suits. Advocacy groups have been focusing more and more of their attention on implementing the law's "mainstreaming" provision, which calls for placement in the least restrictive environment (LRE).

"To the maximum extent appropriate, handicapped children, including children in public or private institutions or other care facilities, [must be] educated with children who are not handicapped," P.L. 94-142 mandates.

A number of advocacy lawyers say LRE has not been enforced, especially for older children, and the Education Department's 1986 report to Congress on P.L. 94-142 particularly faults implementation of LRE for seriously emotionally disturbed youths.

"There's no way you can bus a mentally retarded child from the warehouse to a public school for six hours a day and get him socialized," said Martin. "What's the good of sending a child to school six hours a day when he's trashed by the other 18 hours?"

"For example, self-toileting: it's very hard to teach six hours a day and then let the kid do what he wants 18 hours a day. Or feeding with utensils" when a child may use his hands at home or be fed by a staff member or by gastronomy tubes, said Martin. "These are kids who could, with proper attention, learn to feed themselves, learn to toilet themselves."

LRE "is an entitlement to be placed in their neighborhood to the maximum extent appropriate, where support systems would exist, and they would be involved in the community as opposed to being shipped to a facility for the handicapped," Boundy said.

Stern said mainstreaming is the crux of the enforcement battle in many districts, including the New York case she monitored, and Mayerson, of DREDF, anticipated more litigation toward integrating handicapped students with their nonhandicapped peers. The law requires schools to have a "compelling educational reason" for segregating students in an institution or in daytime special education centers, she said, but parents often find themselves in the position of proving the child should be mainstreamed, Mayerson maintains.

"Some say integration is just an educational technique, at the discretion of the school district, or that there is a preference for integration, but not a mandate," Mayerson observed. "I feel it's clear" there must be a compelling reason for separation, "but unfortunately it hasn't been implemented that way."

She cited the 1983 6th U.S. Circuit Court of Appeals decision in *Roncker v. Walter* (700 F.2d 1058; cert. denied, 464 U.S. 864), which said integrated placement is mandatory if possible, and the burden of proof for doing otherwise is on the school.

"In a case where the segregated facility is considered superior, the court should determine whether the services which make that placement superior could be feasibly provided in a nonsegregated setting," said the 6th Circuit. "If they can, the placement in the segregated school would be inappropriate under the Act."

* * *

Ironically, Mayerson added, some children miss out on mainstreaming for the sake of another fundamental special education right: related services. Central schools for handicapped students may be the most efficient way to meet special education and related services needs, but the arrangement can backfire against a child, Mayerson said. "Provision of related services [such as therapy available in a special school] is often used to deny integrated placement."

In the same way, providing private or residential placements where appropriate "and the concept of mainstreaming or placement in the least restrictive environment could be seen as contradictory policies," CRS's Jones noted in a 1986 paper on special education law.

"However, they can also be seen as complementary. The two provisions can be seen as reflecting congressional intent to produce a broad definition of what is 'appropriate' placement," that is, placement that provides both education and the opportunity to participate in society, Jones wrote.

Jones said the 3rd Circuit reconciled the principles in 1981 in *Kruelle v. New Castle County School District* (642 F.2d 687). It is clear that if "residential placement is the only realistic option for learning improvement, the question of 'least restrictive' environment is also resolved," said *Kruelle*. If the more restrictive facility is better, the question is whether the public school program can provide the same services feasibly, *Kruelle* said. If so, the private placement would be inappropriate.

Although 93 percent of all handicapped students are educated in at least some regular classes, there have been "persistent problems in providing an appropriate educational program within the LRE for all handicapped children," according to the Education Department's report to Congress.

The department reports that about 7 percent of all handicapped children in the 1983-84 academic year were educated outside of regular school environments, in special schools or at home, and another 25 percent were educated mainly in separate classes within public schools. Both of those groups are obvious candidates for LRE disputes. But disputes can arise even over the placements of the remaining 69 percent of students, who spent most of their time in regular classes with supplementary aids and services. (The total does not add to 100 percent because the figures are rounded.)

With special education advocates concerned about mainstreaming, desegregation suits are a possibility, said Gerry. "There is still massive separation in secondary schools, and even segregation," he said.

But the opposite placement battle occurs frequently, too. Parents sometimes ask the school to pay for a child's institutionalization, while the school believes it can offer a better program in the regular system. While parents say they need or want to put their children in a 24-hour residential placement, the reasons are not always educational, and school districts are not required to pay for any strictly residential portion of the placement.

"The distinctions between care and residential services, who makes what decisions about placement, when the placement is for noneducational services, and who has the primary financial responsibility" need to be resolved, Weintraub said.

AIDS

Students with AIDS have been some of the toughest to place. The syndrome does not automatically make a child handicapped within the meaning of P.L. 94-142, but the argument can be made that when children with AIDS fall under the act, they should be educated in the least restrictive environment.

"For most infected school-age children, the benefits of an unrestricted setting would outweigh the risks of their acquiring potentially harmful infections in the setting and the apparent nonexistent risk of transmission" of the virus that can cause AIDS, state the guidelines published by the federal Centers for Disease Control (CDC).

Given the possibility — however remote — of transmitting AIDS to others, and given the risk an AIDS patient will catch infections from other students, however, school officials must consider each child with AIDS separately. CDC advises a more restricted environment for preschoolers, "for some neurologically handicapped children who lack control of their body secretions or who display behavior such as biting and [for] those children who have uncoverable, oozing lesions."

Jones notes that, balancing the mainstreaming imperative of P.L. 94-142, there are precedents for making an exception to integration where there is a danger to other students. Citing two discipline cases in which students were moved after threatening other students — the 11th Circuit's 1984 ruling in *Victoria L. v. District School Board of Lee County, Fla.* (741 F.2d 369) and *Jackson v. Franklin County, Miss., School Board* (765 F.2d 535) from the 5th Circuit in 1985 — Jones observes that the rationale of the 11th and 5th circuits in those cases could apply to a biting student with AIDS.

The federal district for central California, however, in 1986 issued a preliminary injunction ordering the mainstreaming of a child with AIDS who bit another student. In *Thomas v. Atascadero Unified School District* (No. 86-6609-AHS[BX]) (C.D.Cal. Nov 17, 1986), Ryan Thomas bit another pupil, without breaking the skin, allegedly while a group of other students were bullying him. The school put Thomas in a home instruction program, but the court said that would violate Section 504 of the Rehabilitation Act, which prohibits disability-based discrimination in federally funded programs.

Individual consideration also is required to determine whether a child with AIDS even fits under the P.L. 94-142 rubric. AIDS may accompany other potentially handicapping conditions, such as hemophilia or birth defects related to a mother's drug use while pregnant.

But whether a student with AIDS is handicapped under P.L. 94-142 depends on if the syndrome is hurting his or her educational performance. Madeleine Will, the Education Department's assistant secretary for special education and rehabilitative services, has advised educators to ask, on a case-by-case basis, "What is it about that condition that would require the child to be placed in special education? Is the child cognitively impaired?"

"I think the burden of proof would be on the system of regular education, which needs to identify exactly what it is this child requires that cannot be delivered in the universe of regular education. Because the separation of a child from the world of regular education is a very serious matter, and it should be done only if it's clear the child will benefit," Will said.

Queens County, N.Y., Supreme Court Judge Harold Hyman agreed with that assessment in his 1986 ruling in *District 27 Community School Board v. Board of Education of the City of New York*

(502 N.Y.S.2d 325). A child with AIDS or the less severe condition, AIDS-Related Complex (ARC), "could become handicapped as a result of deterioration in his or her condition," but such children are not handicapped under P.L. 94-142 "merely because they have AIDS/ARC or are infected with the virus," he said.

When Ryan White, an Indiana teenager and hemophiliac with AIDS, was kept out of school and his mother filed suit in 1985 to force a school district to readmit her son, a U.S. district judge in Indianapolis at first treated the case as though White automatically was handicapped under P.L. 94-142 because he had AIDS. Other courts, however, have not followed the lead of *White v. Western School Corp.* (IP 85-1192C), which came in one of the first legal battles over a student with AIDS before the classification issue had been debated.

But even if a student with AIDS is not handicapped under P.L. 94-142, he or she might be handicapped under Section 504 of the Rehabilitation Act, under a 1987 Supreme Court ruling, *School Board of Nassau County v. Arline* (55 U.S.L.W. 4245), that said a contagious disease may be a handicap if the victim is or has been impaired by it or is perceived as impaired. The Section 504 regulations set up educational standards very close to those schools must meet under P.L. 94-142, guaranteeing an "appropriate education" with "regular or special education and related aids and services . . . designed to meet individual educational needs."

Related Services

Despite *Rowley* and *Irving Independent School District v. Tatro* (468 U.S. 883), in which the Supreme Court required a district to have an employee catheterize a student at school, gray areas linger in interpretation of related services.

"It was expected that the definition of related services in the act would suffice, but litigation history shows more clarification is needed," the National Association of State Directors of Special Education said in testimony on the 1986 Education of the Handicapped Act Amendments. In a "free appropriate public education," related services are half the game, with "special education" itself doing the rest.

Encompassing everything from transportation to speech pathology to catheterization, in Amber Tatro's case, related services are those "required to assist a handicapped child to benefit from special education," except for nondiagnostic medical services. The line between medical services schools need not provide and nonmedical services that may be demanded is fuzzy, however, particularly when it comes to psychological services for emotionally disturbed children. "The education and the therapy service are really intertwined, and you can't separate them," said Gerry.

In *Tatro,* the Court stressed that without catheterization, Tatro could not stay at school and would lose access to her education; the decision also relied upon the fact that the service could be done by a nurse or layperson rather than a licensed physician. Because of that, some school lawyers credit *Tatro* with causing lower courts to begin "to acknowledge that school districts are not required to provide medical services," as Bobbie Albanese, counsel to the Orange County, Calif., superintendent, put it.

"However, the courts have struggled with the distinction between a service that is 'purely medical' and one that may qualify as a related service necessary to provide a child with a free appropriate public education," Albanese said in a 1986 paper written for publication by the Council of School Attorneys, an arm of the National School Boards Association (NSBA), and for presentation at the council's 1987 school law seminar.

For example, consider "general intense ongoing psychotherapy for a schizophrenic child," Gerry said. "We're talking about 70, 75, 80, 85 bucks an hour, and kids who need a lot of it." Open-heart surgery also may be necessary for a child to benefit from education but clearly does not qualify, he pointed out. Mayerson added that the circumstances under which a given service is delivered can provoke conflict among legal experts about whether the service qualifies.

Said Warren Kreunen, a Milwaukee attorney who represents school districts in special education cases, "The problem is, psychological treatment [includes] many of the same things psychiatrists do, except prescribing medicine. That's a broad range of things to include."

Even before *Tatro,* the courts have distinguished between mental health services provided by a psychiatrist — a licensed physician — and those that can be performed by others, notes CRS's Jones. Those cases included:

■ *Darlene L. v. Illinois State Board of Education* (568 F.Supp. 1340), in which the federal district court for northern Illinois in 1983 said psychological services by a licensed phsyician are not a related service, but the services of psychologists — who are not medical doctors — can be;

■ the U.S. district court for the District of Columbia's ruling in 1983 in *McKenzie v. Jefferson* (566 F.Supp. 404), saying that a child's psychiatric hospitalization was not a related service if the placement was made for the sake of medical treatment; and

- the 3rd Circuit's 1984 decision in *Piscataway Township Board of Education v. T.G.* (cert. denied, 53 U.S.L.W. 3436), which said psychotherapy for an emotionally disturbed student qualifies as a related service under P.L. 94-142; half a year after *Tatro,* the Supreme Court without comment refused to review it.

But the rules still are not rigidly set, Albanese noted. In a 1986 ruling in *Max M. v. Illinois State Board of Education* (629 F.Supp. 1504), the federal district court for northern Illinois said the nature of the service, not the personnel providing it, determines whether it is a reimbursable related service. But the court added that the district should be held liable for only "the costs of those services as if they had been provided by the minimum level health care provider recognized as competent to perform the related service," Albanese added.

Albanese said she was shocked by two recent cases in which hearing officers ordered districts to pay for psychiatric services provided to students in psychiatric hospitals:

- *Clovis Unified School District v. California Office of Hearings* (CV-F-85-479 EDP), in which the federal district court for eastern California in 1986 upheld the hearing officer's ruling. The case now is on appeal to the 9th U.S. Circuit Court of Appeals (86-2742); and

- *Orange Unified School District v. Boggus* (Nos. 46-97-63 and 47-41-76), which was pending as of March 1987 in the Superior Court of California for Orange County.

On the other hand, in *Detsel v. Auburn Enlarged City School District* (637 F.Supp. 1022), the U.S. district court for northern New York in 1986 said a district did not have to provide constant supervision of a child with severe physical disabilities, even though a doctor was not required for the service. The court said the monitoring amounted to medical care that the district did not have to provide. The regulations on medical services, the court said, quoting *Tatro,* were meant to "spare schools from an obligation to provide a service that might well prove unduly expensive and beyond the range of their competence."

But as *Detsel* shows, the fine line between medical and nonmedical services poses problems aside from psychological services, too. Some decisions "have required school staff to clean out tracheotomy tubes, because these are not medical services requiring a doctor. That's a pretty broad range" of services considered nonmedical, Kreunen said.

"You have school personnel worried about that" and afraid of malpractice liability if, for example, they are called upon to administer emergency medication and err somehow, he said. "The question is, how far must schools go to educate the very severely handicapped?"

The Future Of Special Education Litigation 35

"You're starting to get kids in [breathing equipment] mainstreamed in the classroom," Kreunen said. "The kid may be benefiting, but maybe not as much as possible. And you may start to diminish the education of the other kids in the classroom" by diverting the teacher's energy and the attention of the other students. "That's an unpopular thing to say," Kreunen acknowledged.

* * *

Related services questions come up not only in the psychologist's office but also on the athletic field. In a 1986 ruling in *Rettig v. Kent City, Ohio, School District* (788 F.2d 328; cert. denied, 54 U.S.L.W. 3859), the 6th Circuit said school districts do not have to provide handicapped children with "an equal opportunity" for participating in extracurricular activities, even though a P.L. 94-142 regulation requires that.

Ruling that the regulation is in conflict with *Rowley,* the 6th Circuit said schools only have to ensure that the IEP, "when taken in its entirety, is reasonably calculated to enable the child to receive educational benefits." The court also said the weekly hour of activities that the parents sought in *Rettig* would have provided no significant educational benefits. The Supreme Court let that decision stand.

* * *

The costs of different placement alternatives and related services can be an issue when educators write IEPs. With the determination of an appropriate placement being the first question, it is not common for cost to be an explicit issue in litigation, but it has happened.

"You're starting to see more cases that recognize the validity of cost considerations in public schools," commented Arnold. "Over the past few years I'm beginning to see cases where the judge says, 'Yes, you can consider cost.' That's almost surprising to me."

In *Kruelle,* for example, courts have said cost is a proper factor because excessive spending on one handicapped student deprives other handicapped children of appropriate education funds, or deprives students in regular education classes. The idea is the flip side of the D.C. District Court's reasoning in 1972 in *Mills v. Board of Education of the District of Columbia* (348 F. Supp. 866), which said schools should not withhold spending on handicapped students to spend more on nonhandicapped students.

CLE's Boundy conceded that courts may have become "increasingly aware" of the costs as an issue. But even where cost is great, courts should consider the appropriateness of differently priced options, she said. She quoted a 1984 case, *Clevenger v. Oakridge School Board* (744 F.2d 514), in which the 6th U.S. Circuit Court of Appeals said, "Cost considerations are only relevant when choosing between several options, all of which are for an appropriate education. When only one is appropriate, there is no choice."

The 1986 EHA Amendments

With the 1986 EHA amendments — early intervention for infants and the preschool special education mandate — still in their own infancy, only a sketchy outline of the legal questions they may raise was possible as of March 1987. Some are apparent by analogy to problems in existing preschool and school-age programs, however.

One educator anticipated conflicts over the level of services schools are willing to write into a 3-year-old's IEP. Once a service is in an IEP, it is difficult to drop even if the student outgrows it, and the younger the student is to start, the more likely the special education provided will bring progress that outdates services in the IEP. A district might offer some summer school without prescribing it in the IEP, for example, as a way to avoid making a lengthy and formal commitment to it, said that educator.

Some other questions that have been raised so far include:

■ What does least restrictive environment mean for preschoolers, given that many states and districts do not offer preschool for nonhandicapped students? Must districts make efforts to integrate handicapped preschoolers in Head Start programs or day care centers?

Although the new preschool program incorporates by reference the LRE requirement of P.L. 94-142, Gray Garwood, who was staff director for the House Select Education Subcommittee when it wrote the House version of the amendments, said he sees the requirement as not generally relevant for preschoolers. A district certainly cannot be expected to create a nonhandicapped preschool just for the sake of mainstreaming, he added.

The 8th Circuit, in its 1986 ruling in *Mark and Ruth A. v. Grant Wood Area Education Agency* (795 F.2d 52; cert. denied, March 23, 1987), made the same point in upholding a district's decision to put a preschooler in an all-handicapped classroom in a public school. The parents had advocated placement in a private program designed to integrate handicapped and nonhandicapped students.

■ For infants, is the "individualized family service plan" (IFSP), which states must develop for the family of each child served, a binding contract between the family and state agencies?

■ Does the IFSP continue after the child turns 3? If so, who pays

for family services? Will infants suddenly lose eligibilty for accustomed services on their third birthdays? Will some classified as at risk of developmental delay be edged from the program altogether?
- How will information on infants and families remain confidential in the interagency web?

Also, for infants and toddlers, the new program provides only the skeleton of the P.L. 94-142 due process system and leaves most of the procedures and rights for states to devise. Under P.L. 94-142, Garwood said, "it is clear what the individual has a right to: special education and related services which are definable, identifiable and providable." Services for infants are far less clearly understood, however. "There is no right yet," Garwood said. "Once the states are participating fully, then there can be some other effort" to make sure the due process procedures suffice.

Iowa, which has served all handicapped children from birth since 1980, applied the same P.L. 94-142 due process requirements to its infant program "with a minimum of problems" and controversy, according to Joan Turner Clary, early childhood special education program consultant to the Iowa Department of Education.

Garwood anticipated little litigation under the infants' and preschool programs. Seven years ago the extension of services "would have been a catastrophe, but the system [now] is much better able to absorb this," he said. "It'll just burp and go on with it. I don't think it's going to create as many problems" as some people think.

The Medicaid Conflict

The 1986 amendments to EHA created a new conflict that may have to be resolved in the courts. Congress said state agencies other than the education agency must pay for related services in an IEP if they would have paid for them in the absence of an IEP. The amendments direct states to develop interagency agreements to allocate costs among the various public agencies that have responsibilities for handicapped children.

"That's going to be a really important battleground, and on this issue parents and school systems have exactly the same interests," at last, Gerry said. The provision for reimbursements from other agencies applies to special education for students of all ages, not just the new infant and preschooler provisions. Given the timing of development of the interagency agreements, "the real impact will be felt in the fall of '88," Gerry predicted.

The new interagency agreements must define each agency's financial responsibility and set policies and procedures for resolving disputes, including procedures by which school districts can seek reimbursement for health and social services they provide according to students' IEPs.

"Of course the other agencies aren't going to go down without a fight," Gerry said. "But if you look at the overall structure, that's just not fair to make public schools the deep pocket for every kind of service that child needs."

He expected the "biggest areas" for reimbursement battles to be Medicaid (Title XIX of the Social Security Act) for children from low income families; Community Mental Health; and Vocational Rehabilitation, for which youths become eligible at age 16. Other areas will include Maternal and Child Health Block Grants (Social Security Title V); Early and Periodic Screening, Diagnosis and Treatment; Child Welfare Services; Head Start; and the Developmental Disabilities program.

The 1986 amendments say the state education agency's responsibility for P.L. 94-142 "shall not be construed to limit the responsibility of [other agencies] . . . from providing or paying for some or all of the costs of a free appropriate public education to be provided handicapped children." The amendments add that the EHA "shall not be construed to permit a State to reduce medical and other assistance or to alter eligibility under titles V and XIX of the Social Security Act with respect to the provision of a free appropriate public education."

The biggest fight might be with the federal government, at least under the Reagan administration. The Health and Human Services Department, which runs Medicaid, strongly opposes Medicaid reimbursements for services in an IEP, arguing that position in administrative opinions and in comments on a July 1986 General Accounting Office report on the issue.

Under a Connecticut interagency agreement foreshadowing the 1986 EHA amendments, GAO reported that local school districts receive about $5 million per year in Medicaid reimbursements for school-based health services provided to handicapped children. HHS said the program "ignores long-standing Medicaid statutory provisions, regulations, and the State Medicaid Manual which precludes Federal Medicaid reimbursement where other funding is available." In a September 1985 policy statement in the state manual, HHS's Health Care Financing Administration declared Medicaid coverage unavailable for services described in an IEP.

"Ultimately, it's going to be settled," albeit with "stress, groans and tensions," observed Garwood. Assuming Health and Human Services does not give in and Congress does not amend the Social Security Act—or EHA—to resolve the issue, "somebody's going to file a lawsuit, maybe a school district [unable] to recover funds from other agencies."

There has been one ruling on the issue, in which a federal district court in Massachusetts found residential institutions for mentally retarded students eligible for reimbursement of health services even though the services were educational in that they were listed in an IEP. HHS has appealed that ruling, *Massachusetts v. Heckler* (616 F.Supp. 687), to the 1st Circuit.

Gerry was optimistic that schools would see a tangential benefit in addition to the financial relief once reimbursement is resolved. "A lot of due process hearings have been fights over resources, so if you take some of the financial pressure off school districts, there's a good chance [conflicts] will get resolved without hearings," he said. "If school systems respond creatively, they can turn some disputes into collaborative efforts with parents," although "I'm not saying it's going to solve everything," he added.

The Supreme Court Takes Up Discipline

Another issue that attracted keen attention during 1987 was discipline. P.L. 94-142 says nothing directly about it, leaving parents and educators to read between the lines. Several cases have pitted parents protective of an unruly child's educational placement against district officials afraid the child will hurt someone or disrupt education at the school.

Discipline calls several parts of P.L. 94-142 into play: the procedures for a change of placement, the meaning of "mainstreaming" and of "appropriate" education, and the "stay put" provision keeping the child in her or his current placement until the parents and school agree on a change.

Some advocacy lawyers fear parents' lawsuits are scaring schools away from enforcing needed discipline, and others say schools have too much latitude in disciplining handicapped students. While some school lawyers feel the due process procedures courts have required schools to follow are too strict, an equal problem is that the case law so far does not answer all questions about a school's responsibilities and rights in discipline.

Gwen Gregory, deputy general counsel of NSBA, and others have been hoping for a Supreme Court ruling on the issue, and the Court took a step toward answering their wishes when it agreed to hear a California case regarding suspensions. That case, *Honig v. Doe* (55 U.S.L.W. 3445), is likely to be decided in 1988.

Under the precedents that set the stage for *Honig*, handicapped students, like other pupils, have a right to a hearing if they are to be suspended, under the Supreme Court's 1975 decision in *Goss v. Lopez* (419 U.S. 565). Overturning an Ohio law allowing some suspensions with no hearing, *Goss* said students have a constitutionally protected interest in public education that cannot be revoked without due process.

Goss established minimal due process rights for brief suspensions: the student's right to "notice of the charges against him" and some hearing—"at least an informal give-and-take between student and disciplinarian, preferably prior to the suspension."

The chief discipline ruling for special education followed that lead. In *S-1 v. Turlington* (635 F.2d 342), the 5th Circuit in 1981 held that expulsion of a handicapped student is a change in placement and that, after an expulsion, services cannot cease altogether. The 5th Circuit echoed other courts' opinions that a student cannot be expelled for behavior that is a manifestation of his or her handicap. Since *S-1*, "Short suspensions are generally allowed if there is a danger to other students, but that is a trend, not an absolute," Jones said.

In *Honig v. Doe,* the Supreme Court agreed to decide whether a school may change the placement of a handicapped student who is a danger to him- or herself or others without drafting an entire new education plan for the child. The Court will review a 1986 decision by the 9th Circuit that said districts may suspend handicapped pupils for the duration allowed by state law for their nonhandicapped peers; in California, where *Honig* originated, that is 20 consecutive days or 30 consecutive days for students being transferred to a new placement.

Apart from that suspension, though, a school cannot change a violent student's placement over the parents' objections without adopting a new IEP because doing so would violate P.L. 94-142's stay put provision, the 9th Circuit ruled in the case, then called *Doe v. Maher* (793 F.2d 1470).

Instead, educators confronted with a violent handicapped student may resort to "the gamut of lesser disciplinary measures and program variations that do not rise to the level of changes in placement," the 9th Circuit said. In extraordinary cases in which parents resist an immediate placement change school officials consider imperative, officials may seek a court order, the court added.

California schools chief Bill Honig contends the 9th Circuit's approach could have "disastrous consequences." As parents help draft IEPs and can challenge a school's plan, it can take months or years to put a new IEP in place, he argues.

Toby Fishbein Rubin, a lawyer for the students, was "shocked" that the Court accepted the case. But if the 9th Circuit is affirmed, "the impact will be tremendous for students," she said. Currently, she said, "the easiest way for schools to deal with difficult students is to remove them."

The Future Of Special Education Litigation

The case began in 1980 when an emotionally disturbed student tried to choke another pupil and broke a plate glass window, and a second handicapped student engaged in theft and extortion and made sexual advances on other students. The San Francisco Unified School District suspended both students indefinitely but provided home instruction.

Attorneys for the students contend Honig exaggerates the impact of the 9th Circuit ruling, because that ruling does allow suspensions of as long as 20 days without an IEP evaluation. "The exception sought . . . would override entirely the Congressional purpose behind [P.L. 94-142]: to guarantee an education to handicapped students regardless of the nature or severity of their handicaps," the students' attorneys said, contending Honig wants to give districts "unbridled discretion."

Atlanta school lawyer Charles Weatherly counters that applying the 9th Circuit ruling elsewhere would be even tougher on schools, because most state laws do not allow suspensions as long as 20 days; Georgia's limit is 10 days, he said. Weatherly added that discipline cases account for about half the legal problems he handles.

Arguments in *Honig* may consider the meaning of mainstreaming. "If you look at LRE as an entitlement, how can you justify expelling handicapped children? How can you justify suspensions?" CLE's Boundy has asked. "There is no problem with removal in an emergency. What the regulations and the act don't provide for is this extended exclusion from school," especially through serial suspensions, none of which alone is long enough to justify invoking the due process proceedings for a change of placement.

NSBA's Gregory advocated the opposite approach, a Supreme Court ruling that a suspension or expulsion is not a change of placement. "It's a part of being mainstreamed. They could also say it's an exception [to the stay put rule] that must have been intended because any other reading" would verge on nonsensical, she said.

The possibility of an emergency court order to remove a violent student does not dispense with the practical problems educators face, say school lawyers. "You could have a situation where it's not an emergency in terms of safety, but the kid is so disruptive that no one is learning. It's an educational emergency," Gregory said. She was considering arguing in *Honig* that school officials should have the flexibility to make a quick change of placement even for students who are merely disruptive, not dangerous. If parents object, it can be they who seek judicial intervention, she said.

Gregory thought judges too easily attribute misbehavior to a handicap, an important factor because that connection is what brings

P.L. 94-142 into play during discipline. Although *Honig* does not directly raise the question, Gregory hoped the Court would define more clearly — and more narrowly than some courts have — the relationship between misbehavior and a student's handicap.

She and Weatherly supported the 9th Circuit's application of the stay put rule only to "conduct that is caused by, or has a direct and substantial relationship to, the child's handicap." The 9th Circuit added that "a handicapped child's conduct is covered . . . only if the handicap significantly impairs the child's behavioral controls." That definition "does not embrace conduct that bears only an attenuated relationship to the child's handicap," the court said. The stay put rule would not apply, for example, if a physical handicap causes a child to lose self-esteem, and the child consciously misbehaves to gain the attention, or win the approval, of peers.

"True, an emotionally disturbed kid is going to be more of a discipline problem," Gregory said. "But when you put them in the mainstream program, that's part of the program." The threat of discipline "is a teaching tool: living in society you have to abide by the rules," she added. "Some attorneys suggest you write discipline into the IEP."

Lashing out during an epileptic seizure certainly is related to the handicap, but most cases are less clear, she said. Gregory argued that if the handicapped student "knows the difference between right and wrong and is capable of refraining from the misbehavior," then the student should be disciplined as his or her nonhandicapped peers are. An inflexible rule on discipline from the Supreme Court would only discourage mainstreaming, she said.

Like some school attorneys, Gerry found courts' discipline standards sometimes a bit alarming. "I have this nightmare of a kid running around school stabbing people and they can't take the knife away from him and send him home because he hasn't had a case conference" to see whether he might have a handicap that is responsible for his behavior, he said.

But Gerry suggested that the Supreme Court might allow exceptions to the stay put rule, and he noted that the justices have narrowed the provision before, in a different context. In a 1985 ruling in *Burlington School Committee v. Department of Education* (53 U.S.L.W. 4509), in which parents unilaterally transferred their child to a private school, the Court held that a parental violation of the stay put provision did not waive their right to reimbursement.

"Clearly, after *Burlington*, the stay put provision is in some jeopardy," Gerry said.

Questions are likely to remain even after *Honig*. For example, the courts have not yet dealt with serial suspensions of less than 10 days

The Future Of Special Education Litigation 43

each. Seeing "lots of room for improvement" and for a clear judicial standard, Boundy looked for more judicial restraints in disciplining handicapped students. Suspension or expulsion "is only appropriate when there is an emergency," she said.

It is also not clear whether educational services must be delivered during a suspension; and while *S-1* said services cannot cease altogether after an expulsion, it is not clear what level of service the school system must provide after a child has been expelled.

Appeals court precedents diverging from the 9th Circuit's approach include the 11th Circuit's 1984 ruling in *Victoria L. v. District School Board of Lee County, Fla.* (741 F.2d 369), which invoked the school's duty to provide a safe environment and upheld the immediate transfer of a handicapped student who threatened other pupils with a razor blade.

* * *

Also in *Honig*, the justices will review the 9th Circuit's decision that the state education agency must serve an individual handicapped child directly if that pupil's school district has failed to provide a free appropriate public education. Honig argues P.L. 94-142 requires the state to serve students only when a district is unwilling or unable to operate a special education program or when students "can best be served" by the state—in a school for the deaf, for example. Requiring the state to provide direct services if a district falters in its duties to an individual student would "place an intolerable burden on the states," he contends.

The 9th Circuit, however, said that whenever a district falls short of P.L. 94-142 standards—and the "breach must be significant"—the student "can best be served" by the state. The state has a duty to monitor districts' performance, and the point of monitoring is to ensure the proper services, the court added, finding California's procedures inadequate.

Due Process

On a more routine level than the emergency issues in *Honig v. Doe*, implementation of the procedural safeguards of P.L. 94-142 concerns those on both sides of the courtroom.

"The procedural safeguards of P.L. 94-142 are some of the most significant and most litigated provisions in the Act," CRS's Jones has observed. Important issues include the nature of the due process hearing; mediation; legal avenues of relief for parents and advocacy groups; damages for failure to serve students properly; and the availability of attorneys' fees for parents who prevail in IEP disputes.

Congress settled one of those issues in 1986, including a provision in the Handicapped Children's Protection Act to allow parents to sue not only under P.L. 94-142 but also under civil rights laws such as the Rehabilitation Act, provided they exhaust the administrative hearings first.

The provision reversed the Supreme Court's 1984 ruling in *Smith v. Robinson* (468 U.S. 992), which said P.L. 94-142 was the only avenue for relief in special education cases. By allowing suits under civil rights statutes such as the Rehabilitation Act, HCPA re-broadened the types of special education suits parents can bring, including class action suits, which can be brought under the Rehabilitation Act but not P.L. 94-142.

Another issue on which there has been little guidance is the question whether courts may order compensatory services for inappropriate special education, particularly for students past their 22nd birthdays, the age at which services normally stop. Few courts have ruled on the issue, but the 7th Circuit in a 1983 ruling in *Timms v. Metropolitan School District of Wabash County* (722 F.2d 1310) suggested that such a compensatory damage award may be legitimate. According to CRS's Jones, the few lower courts that have considered compensatory education generally have allowed it. But there is ample room for clarification of the circumstances under which it might be ordered.

Other questions regarding procedural safeguards focus on the administrative due process hearing that parents may request if they object to a proposed change in their child's IEP or if they want a change that the school refuses.

"The IEP is seen as the foundation document" of a child's education, said DREDF's Mayerson. "The biggest problem in practice is that parents can't get anything they want into the IEP" in services, placement or goals. "The school district has the final say. There are so many parents who have to swallow whatever the school districts give them. So a lot of parents are forced into hearings."

Unfortunately, Mayerson said, when the parents reach hearings, some hearing officers will consider only whether the IEP is being implemented, not whether it is appropriate or whether the placement is the least restrictive possible.

Leonard Rieser, an attorney with the Education Law Center in Philadelphia, saw no such problem with the formulation of IEPs or the scope of the hearing examiner's review, but big problems with the hearing process otherwise.

"This 'simple' due process hearing is so complicated that many people simply forgo their rights," Rieser said. "I think the due process hearing is unworkable most of the time, so mediation is a really good option" when parents and schools agree to it voluntarily, he added.

NSBA's Gregory was "troubled" that many hearing examiners informally act as mediators in the due process hearing, effectively making it an extension of the IEP conference. That means that schools—and parents—are pushed to compromise where it is not necessarily in their interests to do that, she said. Hearing officers "won't admit it openly [though], because they're supposed to be judges," she added. Kreunen, however, saw no problem with some hearing officers' attempts to mediate.

CLE's Boundy added more fuel to the fire. All too routinely, she said, hearing examiners are not impartial, and she predicted more attention will focus on that issue in the future.

In 1984, the 11th U.S. Circuit Court of Appeals tackled the impartiality issue head on in *Mayson v. Teague* (749 F.2d 652), Boundy said. The court observed that while a hearing examiner employed in another district or another area of the student's district had no personal interest a case, the officer may well have had professional interests. An examiner may fear retaliation, for example, or set certain standards with the intent that the same standards would be observed in his or her own districts.

Mediation

While there were disagreements about whether hearing examiners should act as mediators, most attorneys supported the growing movement toward mediation at some level, to save on valuable good will as well as on money, time, paperwork and ever costlier liability insurance.

Mediation is taking hold because the due process hearing is "long and complicated, and nobody wins," said Linda Singer, executive director of the Center for Dispute Settlement in Washington, D.C. About 30 states report offering some form of mediation assistance, said Singer, although the standards vary, even within a state, because many programs are locally administered.

Some attorneys were cautious about mediation. Even if no lawyers will be in the hearing room, Boundy said, parents might be smart to talk to a lawyer or legal aide before bargaining away rights they are not even aware of having. Gerry and others stressed that mediation must be voluntary for all parties.

"Formal mediation I have considerably less confidence in," said Gerry. "You can't compromise rights. Either [the mediation] won't be effective, or we'll lose the sense of what the child's rights are." There are times when either the school or the parent should back off from an overly strong demand, he added, and the hope of a mediated compromise may discourage that concession.

On the other hand, Singer said, there may be room for such compromise. "There are enormous gray areas" in what constitutes appropriate education, for example. Also, mediation allows parents "to participate in fashioning the plan," something that may not happen if lawyers take over the case, she said. "Courts are not satisfying people."

Mediation has always played a part, said Pat Wright, director of governmental affairs for DREDF. But it is "not a panacea."

Attorneys' Fees

Of the many issues litigated in this heavily litigated law, one of the most bitter is irrelevant to the handicapped child. That issue, starting not with education but with the due process hearing, is attorneys' fees.

Until 1984, schools routinely were required to pay the legal fees of parents prevailing in IEP disputes. P.L. 94-142 had no "fee-shifting" provision, but courts ordered the payments under other federal rights statutes that do offer fee-shifting provisions.

The Supreme Court brought that to an abrupt stop with its 1984 ruling in Smith, saying P.L. 94-142 is the exclusive route for challenging a school's special education program, and parents therefore could not win fees by augmenting their P.L. 94-142 suits with claims under the Rehabilitation Act, for example.

Congress reversed *Smith* in a pithy bill — HCPA — that fills less than a page of the *Congressional Record,* but not without two years of delay and debate. Much debate concerned the merit of fee awards for work done in the administrative proceedings where parents and schools must begin resolving disagreements. The final version of HCPA, P.L. 99-372, provides for administrative fees.

In the debate before HCPA became law, legislators and school lawyers opposed to administrative fees predicted they would twist educational decisionmaking. Kreunen said that, faced with the threat of lawyers newly attracted to due process hearings, "a lot of schools aren't going to fight. They're going to throw in the towel. It's so expensive that a lot of the smaller districts are reluctant to try these cases." That capitulation is "not always in the best interest of the child," he said.

Just as undesirable, others suspected schools would litigate more. "Look, if we're going to be faced with parents bringing attorneys [to the hearing or even the case conference], our attorneys will be there," one superintendent said. The fear was that "attorneys will do the talking," while parents and school officials "sit in the back," said those cautious about the fees provision.

And the costs of litigation can be numbing. Defending a school district against one family's intricate complaint, Kreunen said he ran up legal fees of close to $20,000, and the parents' fees were probably greater; that case never even came to trial. Fees in a class action are even more impressive. A federal judge in 1986 awarded $200,000 to three attorneys who brought a class action suit against the Rochester, N.Y., City School District and settled it before trial, after a year of negotiations. The city is appealing that award.

With such fears and figures on their minds, school board members fought the administrative fee provision, and no sooner did Congress approve it than their lawyers attacked it on two fronts.

First, although special education advocates consider fees available even if a parent prevails at the administrative level without going to court, many school lawyers say the bill's plain language does not provide for that. Secondly, school lawyers protest the law's retroactivity to *Smith;* the act covers all actions and administrative proceedings pending on or after July 4, 1984.

Plaintiffs have been awarded retroactive fees under HCPA, but as of March 1987 experts knew of no court that had been asked to review the retroactivity. As for cases resolved at the administrative level, no court was known to have dealt with a school arguing the statute did not provide those fees.

It was only a matter of time, though. Within three months of HCPA's passage, school lawyers had marshalled their arguments in two thorough articles in *Inquiry & Analysis,* the newsletter of the Council of School Attorneys.

Authors of HCPA "may very well have intended to provide attorneys' fees to parents who prevail in due process hearings," Fort Lauderdale, Fla., attorney John Bowen notes in an article in the September 1986 issue. "But such an intent does not create a right unless it is somehow expressed in the law."

"In any action or proceeding brought under this subsection," HCPA says, "the court" may award fees. Bowen notes that the subsection of P.L. 94-142 in question—subsection (e) of Section 1415—concerns court actions and state administrative appeals from hearing decisions, not due process hearings themselves; the section does not provide fees for those prevailing in due process hearings, he contends.

Gray Garwood, who directed House work on HCPA, sounds slightly exasperated when he is asked about that argument. "Despite that obscure . . . reference" to different subsections of P.L. 94-142, "it is clear from the legislative history and the language of the [HCPA] statute that parents who prevail at the administrative level" without going to court may win fees, he says.

Henry Cohen, a legislative attorney with CRS, agrees, and he argues that legislators on both sides of the debate over fees for proceedings understood that.

In a September 1986 CRS paper, Cohen concludes that while the reference to subsection (e) arguably precludes fees for hearings, that reference likely "would be regarded by the courts as loose wording that should not be construed narrowly to defeat the clear purpose of the Act."

Bowen also focuses on the words "the court" and says they mean hearing officers cannot award fees. And parents who have prevailed in IEP hearings cannot get around that by going to court for fees alone, Bowen argues, because neither P.L. 94-142 nor HCPA provides for such a visit.

NSBA staff attorney Naomi Gittens, in a later *Inquiry & Analysis* article, argues the Supreme Court followed the same reasoning in a November 1986 ruling denying administrative fees under Title VI of the 1964 Civil Rights Act.

But critics of the argument say that ruling, *North Carolina v. Crest Street Community Council* (55 U.S.L.W. 4001), is irrelevant because administrative hearings are optional under Title VI but not under P.L. 94-142. It makes sense to deny fees for an optional proceeding, they say.

CRS's Cohen adds that parents arguably could sue to recover fees alone because P.L. 94-142 allows suits "under" the statute, not necessarily suits "to enforce" the statute. If the Courts reject that argument, Cohen added in a November 1986 paper on *Crest Street,* then HCPA's legislative history "apparently would be the only basis for construing EHA to permit court actions solely to recover attorneys' fees incurred in administrative proceedings."

Cohen and other critics of those statutory construction arguments emphasize the words "action or proceeding" and quote Rep. Pat Williams, D-Mont., chairman of the Select Education Subcommittee during action on HCPA, who said the "proceeding" is the due process hearing.

Gerry went further. "I don't think the [statutory construction] argument passes the 'risibility test,'" he said, referring to one of the first legal standards lawyers learn: an argument must be deliverable without making everyone laugh. The argument against HCPA's retroactivity, on the other hand, "has a glimmer of respectability," Gerry said.

Gittens argues the retroactivity is unconstitutional. The Supreme Court has said that when Congress ties program funding to compliance with certain conditions, "these conditions must be unambiguously stated so that a state may be aware of the contract terms before making a decision as to whether to enter into the agreement," Gittens noted in the November 1986 *Inquiry & Analysis*. Even if HCPA were retroactive, it cannot be used to reopen orders denying fees before HCPA passed on Aug. 5, 1986, she argues.

But Cohen contends in a January 1987 CRS paper that HCPA's retroactivity is legitimate because potential liability for legal fees came as no surprise.

School officials are putting HCPA's retroactivity to the test in *Georgia Association of Retarded Citizens v. McDaniel* (78-1950) in U.S. district court in northern Georgia and in *Barbara R. v. Tirozzi* (Civ. Action No. H-83-991-PCD) in federal district court in Connecticut.

* * *

Those issues aside, HCPA will give districts and parents new grounds for conflict, Advocacy Inc.'s Martin predicts. For example, the law denies fees to parents who have "unreasonably protracted the final resolution of the controversy." Even if parents protract the proceedings, however, schools may have to pay if their officials also drag the case out.

The IEP hearing "can be nasty enough," Martin says. "I can't wait to see the proceeding over who 'unreasonably protracted' more." Also, parents may win some but not all the points they raise, making it difficult to determine who prevailed or what legal time was spent on each claim. Those provisions "contain some ambiguities which will most likely be clarified by judicial action," Jones predicts.

* * *

Meanwhile, tentative and anecdotal assessments of life under HCPA are surfacing. As some districts review all IEPs at year's end, rather than staggering them throughout the year, the jury was still out in March on the impact of the fees. But half a year after its passage, "The statute has had a significant impact already," Gerry said. It is "beginning to change the climate in which school districts make decisions." From witnessing a few instances he hopes indicate a trend, Gerry said "you don't get that defiant, 'we're going to take this thing all the way up' [attitude]. There is more of a conciliatory tone; officials less automatically go to a hearing" for a decision on their disagreements with parents.

Not all school attorneys dislike the fee law or think it will distort parental involvement or bring about "the Armageddon that some people had projected," as one lawyer said.

On the other hand, another lawyer who preferred not to be named commented, "When HCPA passed, I said we ought to get [our state] to pull out of the federal program; forget the due process" procedures mandated by P.L. 94-142 and provide special education without them.

"I'm not sure due process—when everybody is at each other's throats—is benefiting the kids," that attorney added. Special education conferences originally were not envisioned with lawyers in on the process, but lawyers will be there more often when fees are available for administrative cases.

The Shortcomings Of Litigation

Lawyers and advocates alike say litigation is not always in a child's best interests, and court can be a bad place to settle disputes.

"The legal aspect [of P.L. 94-142] tends to make very bitter adversaries out of parents and administrators," said Kenneth Brown, executive director of special education at the Spring Branch School District in Houston. "When someone names you in a federal lawsuit, you don't feel like going out to dinner with them."

Litigation can exacerbate a situation that is too prone to being adversarial in the first place. Some school attorneys talk about parents manipulating educators and judges with "the tyranny of tears." In a 1986 report, Will, of the Education Department, notes that the decision of a student's placement can be a "battleground. Parents naturally want the best for their children, a desire that leads some parents to interpret rigid rules and eligibility requirements of special programs as indications that school officials are unwilling to help."

"For their part, schools are often ready to fall back on the stereotype of the 'pushy parent,' especially when requests for services and the insistence on a stronger voice in decisionmaking create inconvenience, embarrassment, and confusion," Will wrote in "Educating Students with Learning Problems—A Shared Responsibility." "As a result, a potential partnership is turned into a series of adversarial, hit-and-run encounters."

"These are emotional cases," said Kreunen. "I've had judges with handicapped children [in special education cases], and they won't excuse themselves from the case. The sympathy factor is worked to the hilt." And while sympathy for a handicapped child may be used, ultimately, Kreunen said, "the bill tends more to be a parents' rights bill than a handicapped children's rights bill."

"The lawyer represents his client and the client is that child, not the parent," Gerry agreed. "I think lawyers [on both sides] ought to point this out more. The child often has to go back to the same school afterward."

People should ask themselves, "'What is the environment going to be like for the child in that building, with that principal?' You have to look at the realistic effect on the child, and I don't see that very often," concluded Gerry. "It is a good area to demonstrate that the legal resolution of human problems should be a last resort."

Appendix
Education Of The Handicapped Act

Education Of The Handicapped Act

Part A — General Provisions

SHORT TITLE; STATEMENT OF FINDINGS AND PURPOSE

Sec. 601. (a) This title may be cited as the "Education of the Handicapped Act".

(b) The Congress finds that —

(1) there are more than eight million handicapped children in the United States today;

(2) the special educational needs of such children are not being fully met;

(3) more than half of the handicapped children in the United States do not receive appropriate educational services which would enable them to have full equality of opportunity;

(4) one million of the handicapped children in the United States are excluded entirely from the public school system and will not go through the educational process with their peers;

(5) there are many handicapped children throughout the United States participating in regular school programs whose handicaps prevent them from having a successful educational experience because their handicaps are undetected;

(6) because of the lack of adequate services within the public school system, families are often forced to find services outside the public school system, often at great distance from their residence and at their own expense;

(7) developments in the training of teachers and in diagnostic and instructional procedures and methods have advanced to the point that, given appropriate funding, State and local educational agencies can and will provide effective special education and related services to meet the needs of handicapped children;

(8) State and local educational agencies have a responsibility to provide education for all handicapped children, but present financial resources are inadequate to meet the special educational needs of handicapped children; and

(9) it is in the national interest that the Federal Government

assist State and local efforts to provide programs to meet the educational needs of handicapped children in order to assure equal protection of the law.

(c) It is the purpose of this Act to assure that all handicapped children have available to them, within the time periods specified in section 612(2)(b), a free appropriate public education which emphasizes special education and related services designed to meet their unique needs, to assure that the rights of handicapped children and their parents or guardians are protected, to assist States and localities to provide for the education of all handicapped children, and to assess and assure the effectiveness of efforts to educate handicapped children. *(20 USC 1401)*

DEFINITIONS

SEC. 602. (a) As used in this title—

(1) The term "handicapped children" means mentally retarded, hard of hearing, deaf, speech or language impaired, visually handicapped, seriously emotionally disturbed, orthopedically impaired, or other health impaired children or children with specific learning disabilities who by reason thereof require special education and related services.

(2) (P.L. 98-199, sec. 2(2), repealed this paragraph which defined the term "Commissioner." That law further amended this Act by replacing all references to "Commissioner" or "Commissioner's" with "Secretary" or "Secretary's", respectively.)

(3) The term "Advisory Committee" means the National Advisory Committee on the Education of Handicapped Children.

(4) The term "construction", except where otherwise specified, means (A) erection of new or expansion of existing structures, and the acquisition and installation of equipment therefor; or (B) acquisition of existing structures not owned by any agency or institution making application for assistance under this title; or (C) remodeling or alteration (including the acquisition, installation, modernization, or replacement of equipment) of existing structures; or (D) acquisition of land in connection with the activities in clauses (A), (B), and (C); or (E) a combination of any two or more of the foregoing.

(5) The term "equipment" includes machinery, utilities, and built-in equipment and any necessary enclosures or structures to house them, and includes all other items necessary for the functioning of a particular facility as a facility for the provision of educational services, including items such as instructional equipment and necessary furniture, printed, published, and audio-visual instructional materials, telecommunications, sensory, and other technological aids and devices, and books, periodicals, documents, and other related materials.

(6) The term "State" means any of several States, the District of Columbia, the Commonwealth of Puerto Rico, the Virgin Islands, Guam, American Samoa, the Northern Marianna Islands, or the

Trust Territory of the Pacific Islands.

(7) The term "State educational agency" means the State board of education or other agency or officer primarily responsible for the State supervision of public elementary and secondary schools, or, if there is no such officer or agency, an officer or agency designated by the Governor or by State law.

(8) The term "local educational agency" means a public board of education or other public authority legally constituted within a State for either administrative control or direction of, or to perform a service function for public elementary or secondary schools in a city, county, township, school district, or other political subdivision of a State, or such combination of school districts or counties as are recognized in a State as an administrative agency for its public elementary or secondary schools. Such term also includes any other public institution or agency having administrative control and direction of a public elementary and secondary school.

(9) The term "elementary school" means a day or residential school which provides elementary education, as determined under State law.

(10) The term "secondary school" means a day or residential school which provides secondary education, as determined under State law, except that it does not include any education provided beyond grade 12.

(11) The term "institution of higher education" means an educational institution in any State which —

(A) admits as regular students only individuals having a certificate of graduation from a high school, or the recognized equivalent of such a certificate;

(B) is legally authorized within such State to provide a program of education beyond high school;

(C) provides an educational program for which it awards a bachelor's degree, or provides not less than a two-year program which is acceptable for full credit toward such a degree, or offers a two-year program in engineering, mathematics, or the physical or biological sciences which is designed to prepare the student to work as a technician and at a semiprofessional level in engineering, scientific, or other technological fields which require the understanding and application of basic engineering, scientific, or mathematical principles or knowledge;

(D) is a public or other nonprofit institution;

(E) is accredited by a nationally recognized accrediting agency or association listed by the Secretary pursuant to this paragraph or, if not so accredited, is an institution whose credits are accepted, on transfer, by not less than three institutions which are so accredited, for credit on the same basis as it transferred from an institution so accredited: *Provided, however,* That in the case of an institution offering a two-year program in engineering mathematics, or the physical or biological sciences which is designed to prepare the student to work as a technician and at a semiprofessional level in engineering, scientific, or technological fields which require the understanding and application of basic engineering, scientific, or mathematical principles of knowledge, if the Secretary determines that there is no nationally recognized accrediting agency or association qualified to accredit such institutions, he shall appoint an advisory committee, composed of persons specially qualified to evaluate training provided by such institutions to participate under this Act and shall also determine whether particular institutions meet such standards. For the purposes of this paragraph the Secretary shall publish a list of nationally recognized accrediting agencies or associations which he determines to be reliable authority as to the quality of education or training offered; and

(F) The term includes community colleges receiving funding from the Secretary of the Interior under Public Law 95-471. *(20 USC 1801 note)*

(12) The term "nonprofit" as applied to a school, agency, organization, or institution means a school, agency, organization, or institution owned and operated by one or more nonprofit corporations or associations no part of the net earnings of which inures, or may lawfully inure, to the benefit of any private shareholder or individual.

(13) The term "research and related purposes" means research, research training (including the payment of stipends and allowances), surveys, or demonstrations in the field of education of handicapped children, or the dissemination of information derived therefrom, including (but without limitation) experimental schools.

(14) The term "Secretary" means the Secretary of Education.

(15) The term "children with specific learning disabilities" means those children who have a disorder in one or more of the basic psychological processes involved in understanding or in using language, spoken or written, which disorder may manifest itself in imperfect ability to listen, think, speak, read, write, spell, or do mathematical calculations. Such disorders include such conditions as perceptual handicaps, brain injury, minimal brain disfunction, dyslexia, and developmental aphasia. Such term does not include children who have learning problems which are primarily the result of visual, hearing, or motor handicaps, of mental retardation, of emotional disturbance, or of environmental, cultural, or economic disadvantage.

(16) The term "special education" means specially designed instruction, at no cost to parents or guardians, to meet the unique needs of a handicapped child, including classroom instruction, instruction in physical education, home instruction, and instruction in hospitals and institutions.

(17) The term "related services" means transportation, and such

developmental, corrective, and other supportive services (including speech pathology and audiology, psychological services, physical and occupational therapy, recreation, and medical and counseling services, except that such medical services shall be for diagnostic and evaluation purposes only) as may be required to assist a handicapped child to benefit from special education, and includes the early identification and assessment of handicapping conditions in children.

(18) The term "free appropriate public education" means special education and related services which (A) have been provided at public expense, under public supervision and direction, and without charge, (B) meet the standards of the State educational agency, (C) include an appropriate preschool, elementary, or secondary school education in the State involved, and (D) are provided in conformity with the individualized education program required under section 614(a)(5).

(19) The term "individualized education program" means a written statement for each handicapped child developed in any meeting by a representative of the local educational agency or an intermediate educational unit who shall be qualified to provide, or supervise the provision of, specially designed instruction to meet the unique needs of handicapped children, the teacher, the parents or guardian of such child, and, whenever appropriate, such child, which statement shall include (A) a statement of the present levels of educational performance of such child, (B) a statement of annual goals, including short-term instructional objectives, (C) a statement of the specific educational services to be provided to such child, and the extent to which such child will be able to participate in regular educational programs, (D) the projected date for initiation and anticipated duration of such services, and (E) appropriate objective criteria and evaluation procedures and schedules for determining, on at least an annual basis, whether instructional objectives are being achieved.

(20) The term "excess costs" means those costs which are in excess of the average annual per student expenditure in a local educational agency during the preceding school year for an elementary or secondary school student, as may be appropriate, and which shall be computed after deducting (A) amounts received under this part or under title I or title VII of the Elementary and Secondary Education Act of 1965, and (B) any State or local funds expended for programs which would qualify for assistance under this part or under such titles.

(21) The term "native language" has the meaning given that term by section 703(a)(2) of the Bilingual Education Act (20 U.S.C. 880b-1(a)(2)).

(22) The term "intermediate educational unit" means any public authority, other than a local educational agency, which is under the general supervision of a State educational agency, which is

established by State law for the purpose of providing free public education on a regional basis, and which provides special education and related services to handicapped children within that State.

(b) For purposes of part C of this title, "handicapped youth" means any handicapped child (as defined in section 602(a)(1)) who —
    (1) is twelve years of age or older; or
    (2) is enrolled in the seventh or higher grade in school.

(23)(A) The term "public or private nonprofit agency or organization" includes an Indian tribe.

(B) The terms "Indian", "American Indian", and "Indian American" mean an individual who is a member of an Indian tribe.

(C) The term "Indian tribe" means any Federal or State Indian tribe, band, rancheria, pueblo, colony, or community, including any Alaskan native village or regional village corporation (as defined in or established under the Alaska Native Claims Settlement Act). *(20 USC 1401)*

OFFICE OF SPECIAL EDUCATION PROGRAMS

SEC. 603. (a) There shall be, within the Office of Special Education and Rehabilitative Services in the Department of Education, an Office of Special Education Programs which shall be the principal agency in the Department for administering and carrying out this Act and other programs and activities concerning the education and training of the handicapped.

(b)(1) The Office established under subsection (a) shall be headed by a Deputy Assistant Secretary who shall be selected by the Secretary and shall report directly to the Assistant Secretary for Special Education and Rehabilitative Services. The position of Deputy Assistant Secretary shall be in grade GS-18 of the General Schedule under section 5104 of title 5, United States Code, and shall be a Senior Executive Service position for the purposes of section 3132(a)(2) of such title.

(2) In addition to such Deputy Assistant Secretary, there shall be established in such office not less than six positions for persons to assist the Deputy Assistant Secretary, including the position of Associate Deputy Assistant Secretary. Each such position shall be in grade GS-15 of the General Schedule under section 5104 of title 5, United States Code. *(20 USC 1402)*

ACQUISITION OF EQUIPMENT AND CONSTRUCTION OF NECESSARY FACILITIES

SEC. 605. (a) In the case of any program authorized by this title, if the Secretary determines that such program will be improved by permitting the funds authorized for such program to be used for the acquisition of equipment and the construction of necessary facilities, he may authorize the use of such funds for such purposes.

(b) If within twenty years after the completion of any construction (except minor remodeling or alteration) for which funds have been paid pursuant to a grant or contract under this title the facility constructed ceases to be used for the purposes for which it was constructed, the United States, unless the Secretary determines that there is good cause for releasing the recipient of the funds from its obligation, shall be entitled to recover from the applicant or other owner of the facility an amount which bears the same ratio to the then value of the facility as the amount of such Federal funds bore to the cost of the portion of the facility financed with such funds. Such value shall be determined by agreement of the parties or by action brought in the United States district court for the district in which the facility is situated. *(20 USC 1404)*

EMPLOYMENT OF HANDICAPPED INDIVIDUALS

SEC. 606. The Secretary shall assure that each recipient of assistance under this Act shall make positive efforts to employ and advance in employment qualified handicapped individuals in programs assisted under this Act. *(20 USC 1405)*

GRANTS FOR THE REMOVAL OF ARCHITECTURAL BARRIERS

SEC. 607. (a) The Secretary is authorized to make grants and to enter into cooperative agreements with the Secretary of the Interior with State educational agencies to assist such agencies in making grants to local educational agencies or intermediate educational units to pay part or all of the cost of altering existing buildings and equipment in accordance with standards promulgated under the Act approved August 12, 1968 (Public Law 90-480), relating to architectural barriers.

(b) For the purposes of carrying out the provisions of this section, there are authorized to be appropriated such sums as may be necessary. *(20 USC 1406)*

REQUIREMENTS FOR PRESCRIBING REGULATIONS

SEC. 608. (a) For purposes of complying with section 431(b) of the General Education Provisions Act with respect to regulations promulgated under part B of this Act, the thirty-day period under such section shall be ninety days.

(b) The Secretary may not implement, or publish in final form, any regulation prescribed pursuant to this Act which would procedurally or substantively lessen the protections provided to handicapped children under this Act, as embodied in regulations in effect on July 20, 1983 (particularly as such protections relate to parental consent to initial evaluation or initial placement in special education, least restrictive environment, related services, timelines, attendance of evaluation personnel at IEP meetings, or qualifications of personnel), except to the extent that such regulation reflects the clear and unequivocal intent of the Congress in legislation.

(c) The Secretary shall transmit a copy of any regulations promulgated under this Act to the National Advisory Committee on the Education of the Handicapped concurrently with publication in the Federal Register. *(20 USC 1407)*

ELIGIBILITY FOR FINANCIAL ASSISTANCE

SEC. 609. Effective for fiscal years for which the Secretary may make grants under section 619(b)(1), no State or local educational agency or intermediate educational unit or other public institution or agency may receive a grant under parts C through G which relate exclusively to programs, projects, and activities pertaining to children aged three to five, inclusive, unless the State is eligible to receive a grant under section 619(b)(1).

PART B — ASSISTANCE FOR EDUCATION OF ALL HANDICAPPED CHILDREN

SETTLEMENTS AND ALLOCATIONS

SEC. 611. (a)(1) Except as provided in paragraph (3) and in section 619, the maximum amount of the grant to which a State is entitled under this part for any fiscal year shall be equal to—

(A) the number of handicapped children aged 3-5, inclusive, in a State who are receiving special education and related services as determined under paragraph (3) if the State is eligible for a grant under section 619 and the number of handicapped children aged 6-21, inclusive, in a State who are receiving special education and related services as so determined."
(20 USC 1419)
multiplied by—

(B)(i) 5 per centum, for the fiscal year ending September 30, 1978, of the average per pupil expenditure in public elementary and secondary schools in the United States.

(ii) 10 per centum, for the fiscal year ending September 30, 1979, of the average per pupil expenditure in public elementary and secondary schools in the United States;

(iii) 20 per centum, for the fiscal year ending September 30, 1980, of the average per pupil expenditure in public elementary and secondary schools in the United States;

(iv) 30 per centum, for the fiscal year ending September 30, 1981, of the average per pupil expenditure in public elementary and secondary schools in the United States; and

(v) 40 per centum, for the fiscal year ending September 30, 1982, and for each fiscal year thereafter, of the average per pupil expenditure in public elementary and secondary schools in the United States;

except that no State shall receive an amount which is less than the amount which such State received under this part for the fiscal year ending September 30, 1977.

Education Of The Handicapped Act 63

(2) For the purpose of this subsection and subsection (b) through subsection (e), the term "State" does not include Guam, American Samoa, the Virgin Islands, the Northern Mariana Islands, and the Trust Territory of the Pacific Islands.

(3) The number of handicapped children receiving special education and related services in any fiscal year shall be equal to the average of the number of such children receiving special education and related services on October 1 and February 1 of the fiscal year preceding the fiscal year for which the determination is made.

(4) For purposes of paragraph (1)(B), the term "average per pupil expenditure", in the United States, means the aggregate current expenditures, during the second fiscal year preceding the fiscal year for which the computation is made (or, if satisfactory data for such year are not available at the time of computation, then during the most recent preceding fiscal year for which satisfactory data are available) of all local educational agencies in the United States (which, for purposes of this subsection, means the fifty States and the District of Columbia), as the case may be, plus any direct expenditures by the State for operation of such agencies (without regard to the source of funds from which either of such expenditures are made), divided by the aggregate number of children in average daily attendance to whom such agencies provided free public education during such preceding year.

(5)(A) In determining the allotment of each State under paragraph (1), the Secretary may not count—

(i) handicapped children aged three to seventeen, inclusive, in such State under paragraph (1)(A) to the extent the number of such children is greater than 12 percent of the number of all children aged three to seventeen, inclusive, in such State and the State serves all handicapped children aged three to five, inclusive, in the State pursuant to State law or practice or the order of any court,

(ii) handicapped children aged five to seventeen, inclusive, in such State under paragraph (1)(A) to the extent the number of such children is greater than 12 percent of the number of all children aged five to seventeen, inclusive, in such State and the States does not serve all handicapped children aged three to five inclusive, in the State pursuant to State law or practice on the order of any court; and

(iii) handicapped children who are counted under section 121 of the Elementary and Secondary Education Act of 1965.

(20 USC 2731)

(B) For purposes of subparagraph (A), the number of children aged five to seventeen, inclusive, in any State shall be determined by the Secretary on the basis of the most recent satisfactory data available to him.

(b)(1) Of the funds received under subsection (a) by any State for the fiscal year ending September 30, 1978—

(A) 50 per centum of such funds may be used by such State in accordance with the provisions of paragraph (2); and

(B) 50 per centum of such funds shall be distributed by such State pursuant to subsection (d) to local educational agencies and intermediate educational units in such State, for use in accordance with the priorities established under section 612(3).

(2) Of the funds which any State may use under paragraph (1)(A)—

(A) an amount which is equal to the greater of—

(i) 5 per centum of the total amount of funds received under this part by such State; or

(ii) $200,000;

may be used by such State for administrative costs related to carrying out sections 612 and 613;

(B) the remainder shall be used by such State to provide support services and direct services in accordance with the priorities established under section 612(3).

(c)(1) Of the funds received under subsection (a) by any State for the fiscal year ending September 30, 1979, and for each fiscal year thereafter—

(A) 25 per centum of such funds may be used by such State in accordance with the provisions of paragraph (2); and

(B) except as provided in paragraph (4), 75 per centum of such funds shall be distributed by such State pursuant to subsection (d) to local educational agencies and intermediate educational units in such State, for use in accordance with priorities established under section 612(3).

(2)(A) Subject to the provisions of subparagraph (B), of the funds which any State may use under paragraph (1)(A)—

(i) an amount which is equal to the greater of—

(I) 5 per centum of the total amount of funds received under this part by such State; or

(II) $300,000;

may be used by such State for administrative costs related to carrying out the provisions of sections 612 and 613; and

(ii) the part remaining after use in accordance with clause (i) shall be used by the State (I) to provide support services and direct services in accordance with the priorities estabilshed under section 612(3), and (II) for the administrative costs of monitoring and complaint investigation but only to the extent that such costs exceed the costs of administration incurred during fiscal year 1985. *(20 USC 1412)*

(B) The amount expended by any State from the funds available to such State under paragraph (1)(A) in any fiscal year for the provision of support services or for the provision of direct services shall be matched on a program basis by such State, from funds other than Federal funds, for the provision of support services or the provision of direct services for the fiscal year involved.

Education Of The Handicapped Act

(3) The provisions of section 613(a)(9) shall not apply with respect to amounts available for use by any State under paragraph (2).

(4)(A) No funds shall be distributed by any State under this subsection in any fiscal year to any local educational agency or intermediate educational unit in such State if—

(i) such local educational agency or intermediate educational unit is entitled, under subsection (d), to less than $7,500 for such fiscal year; or

(ii) such local educational agency or intermediate educational unit has not submitted an application for such funds which meets the requirements of section 614.

(B) Whenever the provisions of subparagraph (A) apply, the State involved shall use such funds to assure the provision of a free appropriate education to handicapped children residing in the area served by such local educational agency or such intermediate educational unit. The provisions of paragraph (2)(B) shall not appy to the use of such funds.

(d) From the total amount of funds available to local educational agencies and intermediate educational units in any State under subsection (b)(1)(B) or subsection (c)(1)(B), as the case may be, each local educational agency or intermediate educational unit shall be entitled to an amount which bears the same ratio to the total amount available under subsection (b)(1)(B) or subsection (c)(1)(B), as the case may be, as the number of handicapped children aged three to twenty-one, inclusive, receiving special education and related services in such local educational agency or intermediate educational unit bears to the aggregate number of handicapped children aged three to twenty-one, inclusive, receiving special education and related services in all local educational agencies and intermediate educational units which apply to the State educational agency involved for funds under this part.

(e)(1) The jurisdictions to which this subsection applies are Guam, American Samoa, the Virgin Islands, the Northern Mariana islands, and the Trust Territory of the Pacific Islands.

(2) Each jurisdiction to which this subsection applies shall be entitled to a grant for the purposes set forth in section 601(c) in an amount equal to an amount determined by the Secretary in accordance with criteria based on respective needs, except that the aggregate of the amount to which such jurisdictions are so entitled for any fiscal year shall not exceed an amount equal to 1 per centum of the aggregate of the amounts available to all States under this part for that fiscal year. If the aggregate of the amounts, determined by the Secretary pursuant to the preceding sentence, to be so needed for any fiscal year exceeds an amount equal to such 1 per centum limitation, the entitlement of each such jurisdiction shall be reduced proportionately until such aggregate does not exceed such 1 per centum limitation.

(3) The amount expended for administration by each jurisdiction

under this subsection shall not exceed 5 per centum of the amount allotted to such jurisdiction for any fiscal year, or $35,000, whichever is greater.

(f)(1) The Secretary shall make payments to the Secretary of the Interior according to the need for assistance for the education of handicapped children on reservations serviced by elementary and secondary schools operated for Indian children by the Department of the Interior. The amount of such payment for any fiscal year shall be 1.25 percent of the aggregate amounts available to all States under this section for that fiscal year.

(2) The Secretary of the Interior may receive an allotment under paragraph (1) only after submitting to the Secretary an application which —

(A) meets the applicable requirements of sections 612, 613, and 614(a), *(20 USC 1412)*

(B) includes satisfactory assurance that all handicapped children aged 3 to 5, inclusive receive a free appropriate public education by or before the 1987-1988 school year, *(20 USC 1414)*

(C) includes an assurance that there are public hearings, adequate notice of such hearings, and an opportunity for comment afforded to members of tribes, tribal governing bodies, and designated local school boards before adoption of the policies, programs, and procedures required under sections 612, 613, and 614(a), and

(D) is approved by the Secretary.

Section 616 shall appy to any such application.*(20 USC 1416)*

(g)(1) If the sums appropriated under subsection (h) for any fiscal year for making payments to States under subsection (a) are not sufficient to pay in full the total amounts which all States are entitled to receive under subsection (a) for such fiscal year, the maximum amounts which all States are entitled to receive under subsection (a) for such fiscal year shall be ratably reduced. In case additional funds become available for making such payments for any fiscal year during which the preceding sentence is applicable, such reduced amounts shall be increased on the same basis as they were reduced.

(2) In the case of any fiscal year in which the maximum amounts for which States are eligible have been reduced under the first sentence of paragraph (2), and in which additional funds have not been made available to pay in full the total of such maximum amounts under the last sentence of such paragraph, the State educational agency shall fix dates before which each local educational agency or intermediate educational unit shall report to the State educational agency or intermediate educational unit, under the provisons of subsection (d), which it estimates that it will expend in accordance with the provisions of this section. The amounts so available to any local educational agency or intermedite educational unit, or any amount which would be available to any other local educational agency or intermediate educational unit if it were to submit a program meeting

the requirements of this part, which the State educational agency determines will not be used for the period of its availability, shall be available for allocation to those local educational agencies or intermediate educational units, in the manner provided by this section, which the State educational agency determines will need and be able to use additional funds to carry out approved programs. *(20 USC 1411)*

(h) For grants under subsection (a) there are authorized to be appropriated such sums as may be necessary.

ELIGIBILITY

SEC. 612. In order to qualify for assistance under this part in any fiscal year, a State shall demonstrate to the Secretary that the following conditions are met:

(1) The State has in effect a policy that assures all handicapped children the right to a free appropriate public education.

(2) The State has developed a plan pursuant to section 613(b) in effect prior to the date of the enactment of the Education for All Handicapped Children Act of 1975 and submitted not later than August 21, 1975, which will be amended so as to comply with the provisions of this paragraph. Each such amended plan shall set forth in detail the policies and procedures which the State will undertake or has undertaken in order to assure that—

(A) there is established (i) a goal of providing full educational opportunity to all handicapped children, (ii) a detailed timetable for accomplishing such a goal, and (iii) a description of the kind and number of facilities, personnel, and services necessary throughout the State to meet such a goal;

(B) a free appropriate public education will be available for all handicapped children between the ages of three and eighteen within the State not later than September 1, 1978, and for all handicapped children between the ages of three and twenty-one within the State not later than Septmber 1, 1980, except that, with respect to handicapped children aged three to five and aged eighteen to twenty-one, inclusive, the requirements of this clause shall not be applied in any State if the application of such requirements would be inconsistent with State law or practice, or the order of any court, respecting public education within such age groups in the State;

(C) all children residing in the State who are handicapped, regardless of the severity of their handicap, and who are in need of special education and related services are identified, located, and evaluated, and that a practical method is developed and implemented to determine which children are currently receiving needed special education and related services and which are children are not currently receiving needed special education and related services;

(D) policies and procedures are established in accordance with detailed criteria prescribed under section 617(c); and

(E) the amendment to the plan submitted by the State required by this section shall be available to parents, guardians, and other members of the general public at least thirty days prior to the date of submission of the amendment to the Commission.

(3) The State has established priorities for providing a free appropriate public education to all handicapped children, which priorities shall meet the timetables set forth in clause (B) of paragraph (2) of this section, first with respect to handicapped children who are not receiving an education, and second with respect to handicapped children, within each disability, with the most severe handicaps who are receiving an inadequate education, and has made adequate progress in meeting the timetables set forth in clause (B) of paragraph (2) of this section.

(4) Each local educational agency in the State will maintain records of the individualized education program for each handicapped children, and such program shall be established, reviewed, and revised as provided in section 614(a)(5).

(5) The State has established (A) procedural safeguards as required by section 615, (B) procedures to assure that, to the maximum extent appropriate, handicapped children, including children in public or private institutions or other care facilities, are educated with children who are not handicapped, and that special classes, separate schooling, or other removal of handicapped children from the regular educational environment occurs only when the nature or severity of the handicap is such that education in regular classes with the use of supplementary aids and services cannot be achieved satisfactorily, and (C) procedures to assure that testing and evaluation materials and procedures utilized for the purposes of evaluation and placement of handicapped children will be selected and administered so as not to be racially or culturally discriminatory. Such materials or procedures shall be provided and administered in the child's native language or mode of communication, unless it clearly is not feasible to do so, and no single procedure shall be the sole criterion for determining an appropriate educational program for a child.

(6) The State educational agency shall be responsible for assuring that the requirements of this part are carried out and that all educational programs for handicapped children with the State including all such programs administered by any other State or local agency, will be under the general supervision of the persons responsible for educational programs for handicapped children in the State educational agency and shall meet educational standards of the State educational agency. This paragraph shall not be construed to limit the responsibility of agencies other than educational agencies in a State from providing or paying for some or all of the costs of a free appropriate public education to be provided handicapped children in the State.

(7) The State shall assure that (A) in carrying out the requirements

Education Of The Handicapped Act

of this section procedures are established for consultation with individuals involved in or concerned with the education of handicapped children, including handicapped individuals and parents or guardians of handicapped children, and (B) there are public hearings, adequate notice of such hearings, and an opportunity for comment available to the general public prior to adoption of the policies, programs, and procedures required pursuant to the provisions of this section and section 613. *(20 USC 1412)*

STATE PLANS

SEC. 613. (a) Any State meeting the eligibility requirements set forth in section 612 and desiring to participate in the program under this part shall submit to the Secretary, through its State educational agency, a State plan at such time, in such manner, and containing or accompanied by such information, as he deems necessary. Each such plan shall—

(1) set forth policies and procedures designed to assure that funds paid to the State under this part will be expended in accordance with the provisions of this part, with particular attention given to the provisions of sections 611(b), 611(c), 611(d), 612(2), and 612(3);

(2) provide that programs and procedures will be established to assure that funds received by the State or any of its political subdivisions under any other Federal program, including section 121 of the Elementary and Secondary Education Act of 1965 (20 U.S.C. 241c-2), section 305(b)(8) of such Act (20 U.S.C. 844a(B)(8)) or its successor authority, and section 122(A)(4)(B) of the Vocational Education Act of 1963 (20 U.S.C. 1262(a)(4)(B)), under which there is specific authority for the provision of assistance for the education of handicapped children, will be utilized by the State, or any of its political subdivisions, only in a manner consistent with the goal of providing a free appropriate public education for all handicapped children, except that nothing in this clause shall be construed to limit the specific requirements of the laws governing such Federal programs;

(3) set forth, consistent with the purposes of this Act, a description of programs and procedures for (A) the development and implementation of a comprehensive system of personnel development which shall include the inservice training of general and special educational instructional and support personnel, detailed procedures to assure that all personnel necessary to carry out the purposes of this Act are appropriately and adequately prepared and trained, and effective procedures for acquiring and disseminating to teachers and administrators of programs for handicapped children significant information derived from educational research, demonstration, and similar projects, and (B) adopting, where appropriate, promising educational practices

and materials development through such projects:
(4) set forth policies and procedures to assure—
   (A) that, to the extent consistent with the number and location of handicapped children in the State who are enrolled in private elementary and secondary schools, provision is made for the participation of such children in the program assisted or carried out under this part by providing for such children special education and related services; and
   (B) that (i) handicapped children in private schools and facilities will be provided special education and related services (in conformance with an individualized educational program as required by this part) at no cost to their parents or guardian, if such children are placed in or referred to such schools or facilities by the State or appropriate local educational agency as the means of carrying out the requirements of this part or any other applicable law requiring the provision of special education and related services to all handicapped children within such State, and (ii) in all such instances the State educational agency shall determine whether such schools and facilities meet standards that apply to State and local educational agencies and that children so served have all the rights they would have if served by such agencies;
(5) set forth policies and procedures which assure that the State shall seek to recover any funds made available under this part for services to any child who is determined to be erroneously classified as eligible to be counted under section 611(a) or section 611(d):
(6) provide satisfactory assurance that the control of funds provided under this part, and title to property derived therefrom, shall be in a public agency for the uses and purposes provided in this part, and that a public agency will administer such funds and property;
(7) provide for (A) making such reports in such form and containing such information as the Secretary may require to carry out his functions under this part, and (B) keeping such records and affording such access thereto as the Secretary may find necessary to assure the correctness and verification of such reports and proper disbursement of Federal funds under this part;
(8) provide procedures to assure that final action with respect to any application submitted by a local educational agency or an intermediate educational unit shall not be taken without first affording the local educational agency or intermediate educational unit involved reasonable notice and opportunity for a hearing;
(9) provide satisfactory assurance that Federal funds made

available under this part (A) will not be commingled with State funds, and (B) will be so used as to supplement and increase the level of Federal, State, and local funds (including funds that are not under the direct control of State or local educational agencies) expended for special education and related services provided to handicapped children under this part and in no case to supplant such Federal, State, and local funds, except that, where the State provides clear and convincing evidence that all handicapped children have available to them a free appropriate public education, the Secretary may waive in part the requirement of this clause if he concurs with the evidence provided by the State;

(10) provide, consistent with procedures prescribed pursuant to section 617(a)(2), satisfactory assurance that such fiscal control and fund accounting procedures will be adopted as may be necessary to assure proper disbursement of, and accounting for, Federal funds paid under this part to the State, including any such funds paid by the State to local educational agencies and intermediate educational units;

(11) provide for procedures for evaluation at least annually of the effectiveness of programs in meeting the educational needs of handicapped children (including evaluation of individualized education programs), in accordance with such criteria that the Secretary shall prescribe pursuant to section 617;

(12) provide that the State has an advisory panel, appointed by the Governor or any other official authorized under State law to make such appointments, composed of individuals involved in or concerned with the education of handicapped children, including handicapped individuals, teachers, parents or guardians of handicapped children, State and local education officials, and administrators of programs for handicapped children, which (A) advises the State educational agency of unmet needs within the State in the education of handicapped children, (B) comments publicly on any rules or regulations proposed for issuance by the State regarding the education of handicapped children and the procedures for distribution of funds under this part, and (C) assists the State in developing and reporting such data and evaluations as may assist the Secretary in the performance of his responsibilities under section 618;

(13) set forth policies and procedures for developing and implementing interagency agreements between the State educational agency and other appropriate State and local agencies to (A) define the financial responsibility of each agency for providing handicapped children and youth with free appropriate education, and (B) resolve interagency disputes, including procedures under which local educational agencies may initiate proceedings under the agreement in order to secure reimbursement from other agencies or otherwise implement the

provisions of the agreement.

(14) policies and procedures relating to the establishment and maintenance of standards to ensure that personnel necessary to carry out the purposes of this part are appropriately and adequately prepared and trained, including —

(A) the establishment and maintenance of standards which are consistent with any State approved or recognized certification, licensing, registration, or other comparable requirements which apply to the area in which he or she is providing special education or related services, and

(B) to the extent such standards are not based on the highest requirements in the State applicable to a specific profession or discipline, the steps the State is taking to require the retraining or hiring of personnel that meet appropriate professional requirements in the State. *(20 USC 1413)*

(b) Whenever a State educational agency provides free appropriate public education for handicapped children, or provides direct services to such children, such State educational agency shall include, as part of the State plan required by subsection (a) of this section, such additional assurances not specified in such subsection (a) as are contained in section 614(a), except that funds available for the provision of such education or services may be expended without regard to the provisions relating to excess costs in section 614(a).

(c) The Secretary shall approve any State plan and any modification thereof which —

(1) is submitted by a State eligible in accordance with section 612; and

(2) meets the requirements of subsection (a) and subsection (b).

The Secretary shall disapprove any State plan which does not meet the requirements of the preceding sentence, but shall not finally disapprove a State plan except after reasonable notice and opportunity for a hearing to the State.

(d)(1) If, on the date of enactment of the Education of the Handicapped Act Amendments of 1983, a State educational agency is prohibited by law from providing for the participation in special programs of handicapped children enrolled in private elementary and secondary schools as required by subsection (a)(4), the Secretary shall waive such requirement, and shall arrange for the provision of service to such children through arrangements which shall be subject to the requirements of subsection (a)(4).

(2)(A) When the Secretary arranges for services pursuant to this subsection, the Secretary, after consultation with the appropriate public and private school officials, shall pay to the provider of such services an amount per child which may not exceed the Federal amount provided per child under this part to all handicapped children enrolled in the State for services for the fiscal year preceding the fiscal year for which the determination is made.

(B) Pending final resolution of any investigation or complaint that could result in a determination under this subsection, the Secretary may withhold from the allocation of the affected State educational agency the amount the Secretary estimates would be necessary to pay the cost of such services.

(C) Any determination by the Secretary under this section shall continue in effect until the Secretary determines that there will no longer be any failure or inability on the part of the State educational agency to meet the requirements of subsection (a)(4).

(3)(A) The Secretary shall not take any final action under this subsection until the State educational agency affected by such action has had an opportunity, for at least 45 days after receiving written notice thereof, to submit written objections and to appear before the Secretary or his designee to show cause why such action should not be taken.

(B) If a State educational agency is dissatisfied with the Secretary's final action after a proceeding under subparagraph (A) of this paragraph, it may, within 60 days after notice of such action, file with the United States court of appeals for the circuit in which such State is located a petition for review of that action. A copy of the petition shall be forthwith transmitted by the clerk of the court to the Secretary. The Secretary thereupon shall file in the court the record of the proceedings on which he based his action, as provided in section 2112 of title 28, United States Code.

(C) The findings of fact by the Secretary, if supported by substantial evidence, shall be conclusive; but the court, for good cause shown, may remand the cause to the Secretary to take further evidence, and the Secretary may thereupon make new or modified findings of fact and may modify his previous action, and shall file in the court the record of the further proceedings. Such new or modified findings of fact shall likewise be conclusive if supported by substantial evidence.

(D) Upon the filing of a petition under subparagraph (B), the court shall have jurisdiction to affirm the action of the Secretary or to set it aside, in whole or in part. The judgment of the court shall be subject to review by the Supreme Court of the United Sates upon certiorari or certification as provided in section 1254 of title 28, United States Code.

(e) This Act shall not be construed to permit a State to reduce medical and other assistance available or to alter eligibility under titles V and XIX of the Social Security Act with respect to the provision of a free appropriate public education for handicapped children within the State. *(42 USC 701)*

APPLICATION

SEC. 614. (a) A local educational agency or an intermediate educational unit which desires to receive payments under section 611(d) for any fiscal year shall submit an application to the appropriate

State educational agency. Such application shall—
(1) provide satisfactory assurance that payments under this part will be used for excess costs directly attributable to programs which—
(A) provide that all children residing within the jurisdiction of the local educational agency or the intermediate educational unit who are handicapped, regardless of the severity of their handicap, and are in need of special education and related services will be identified, located, and evaluated, and provide for the inclusion of a practical method of determining which children are currently receiving needed special education and related services and which children are not currently receiving such education and services;
(B) establish policies and procedures in accordance with detailed criteria prescribed under section 617(c);
(C) establish a goal of providing full educational opportunities to all handicapped children, including—
(i) procedures for the implementation and use of the comprehensive system of personnel development established by the State educational agency under section 613(a)(3);
(ii) the provision of, and the establishment of priorities for providing, a free appropriate public education to all handicapped children, first with respect to handicapped children who are not receiving an education, and second with respect to handicapped children, within each disability, with the most severe handicaps who are receiving an inadequate education;
(iii) the participation and consultation of the parents or guardian of such children; and
(iv) to the maximum extent practicable and consistent with the provisions of section 612(5)(B), the provision of special services to enable such children to participate in regular educational programs;
(D) establish a detailed timetable for accomplishing the goal described in subclause (C); and
(E) provide a description of the kind and number of facilities, personnel, and services necessary to meet the goal described in subclause (C);
(2) provide satisfactory assurance that (A) the control of funds provided under this part, and title to property derived from such funds, shall be in a public agency for the uses and purposes provided in this part, and that a public agency will administer such funds and property, (B) Federal funds expended by local educational agencies and intermediate educational units for programs under this part (i) shall be used to pay only the excess costs directly attributable to the education of

handicapped children, and (ii) shall be used to supplement and, to the extent practicable, increase the level of State and local funds expended for the education of handicapped children, and in no case to supplant such State and local funds, and (C) State and local funds will be used in the jurisdiction of the local educational agency or intermediate educational unit to provide services in program areas which, taken as a whole, are at least comparable to services being provided in areas of such jurisdiction which are not receiving funds under this part;

(3)(A) provide for furnishing such information (which, in the case of reports relating to performance, is in accordance with specific performance criteria related to program objectives), as may be necessary to enable the State educational agency to perform its duties under this part, including information relating to the educational achievement of handicapped children participating in programs carried out under this part; and

(B) provide for keeping such records, and provide for affording such access to such records, as the State educational agency may find necessary to assure the correctness and vertification of such information furnished under subclause (A);

(4) provide for making the application and all pertinent documents related to such application available to parents, guardians, and other members of the general public, and provide that all evaluations and reports required under clause (3) shall be public information;

(5) provide assurances that the local educational agency or intermediate educational unit will establish, or revise, whichever is appropriate, an individualized education program for each handicapped child at the beginning of each school year and will then review and, if appropriate revise, its provisions periodically, but not less than annually;

(6) provide satisfactory assurance that policies and programs established and administered by the local educational agency or intermediate educational unit shall be consistent with the provisions of paragraph (1) through paragraph (7) of section 612 and section 613(a); and

(7) provide satisfactory assurance that the local educational agency or intermediate educational unit will establish and maintain procedural safeguards in accordance with the provisions of sections 612(5)(B), 612(5)(C), and 615.

(b)(1) A State educational agency shall approve any application submitted by a local educational agency or an intermediate educational unit under subsection (a) if the State educational agency determines that such application meets the requirements of subsection (a), except that no such application may be approved until the State plan submitted by such State educational agency under subsection (a) is approved by the Secretary under section 613(c). A State educational agency shall disapprove any application submitted by a local educational agency or an intermediate educational unit under subsection (a) if the State educational agency determines that such application does not meet the requirements of subsection (a).

(2)(A) Whenever a State educational agency, after reasonable notice and opportunity for a hearing, finds that a local educational agency or an intermediate educational unit, in the administration of an application approved by the State educational agency under paragraph (1), has failed to comply with any requirement set forth in such application, the State educational agency, after giving appropriate notice to the local educational agency or the intermediate educational unit, shall—

(i) make no further payments to such local educational agency or such intermediate educational unit under section 620 until the State educational agency is satisfied that there is no longer any failure to comply with the requirement involved; or

(ii) take such finding into account in its review of any application made by such local educational agency or such intermediate educational unit under subsection (a).

(B) The provisions of the last sentence of section 616(a) shall apply to any local educational agency or any intermediate educational unit receiving any notification from a State educational agency under this paragraph.

(3) In carrying out its functions under paragraph (1), each State educational agency shall consider any decision made pursuant to a hearing held under section 615 which is adverse to the local educational agency or intermediate educational unit involved in such decision.

(c)(1) A State educational agency may, for purposes of the consideration and approval of applications under this section, require local educational agencies to submit a consolidated application for payments if such State educational agency determines that any individual application submitted by any such local educational agency will be disapproved because such local educational agency is ineligible to receive payments because of the application of section 611(c)(4)(A)(i) or such local educational agency would be unable to establish and maintain programs of sufficient size and scope to effectively meet the educatinal needs of handicapped children.

(2)(A) In any case in which a consolidated application of local educational agencies is approved by a State educational agency under paragraph (1), the payments which such local educational agencies may receive shall be equal to the sum of payments to which each such local eduational agency would be entitled under section 611(d) if an individual application of any such local educational agency had been approved.

(B) The State educational agency shall prescribe rules and regulations with respect to consolidated applications submitted under this subsection which are consistent with the provisions of paragraph (1) through paragraph (7) of section 612 and section 613(a) and which

Education Of The Handicapped Act 77

provide participating local educational agencies with joint responsibilities for implementing programs receiving payments under this part.

(C) In any case in which an intermediate educational unit is required pursuant to State law to carry out the provisions of this part, the joint responsibilities given to local educational agencies under subparagraph (B) shall not apply to the administration and disbursement of any payments received by such intermediate educational unit. Such responsibilities shall be carried out exclusively by such intermediate educational unit.

(d) Whenever a State educational agency determines that a local educational agency—

(1) is unable or unwilling to establish and maintain programs of free appropriate public education which meet the requirements established in subsection (a);

(2) is unable or unwilling to be consolidated with other local educational agencies in order to establish and maintain such programs; or

(3) has one or more handicapped children who can best be served by a regional or State center designed to meet the needs of such children;

the State educational agency shall use the payments which would have been available to such local educational agency to provide special education and related services directly to handicapped childrn residing in the area served by such local educational agency. The State educational agency may provide such education and services in such manner, and at such locations (including regional or State centers), as it considers appropriate, except that the manner in which such education and services are provided shall be consistent with the requirements of this part.

(e) Whenever a State educational agency determines that a local educational agency is adequately providing a free appropriate public education to all handicapped children residing in the area served by such agency, the State educational agency may reallocate funds (or such portion of those funds as may not be required to provide such education and services) made available to such agency, pursuant to section 611(d), to such other local educational agencies within the State as are not adequately providing special education and related services to all handicapped children residing in the areas served by such other local educational agencies.

(f) Notwithstanding the provisions of subsection (a)(2)(B)(ii), any local educational agency which is required to carry out any program for the education of handicapped children pursuant to a State law shall be entitled to receive payments under section 611(d) for use in carrying out such program, except that such payments may not be used to reduce the level of expenditures for such program made by such local educational agency from State or local funds below the level of such expenditures for the fiscal year prior to the fiscal year

for which such local educational agency seeks such payments.
(20 USC 1414)

PROCEDURAL SAFEGUARDS

SEC. 615. (a) Any State educational agency, any local educational agency, and any intermediate educational unit which receives assistance under this part shall establish and maintain procedures in accordance with subsection (b) through subsection (e) of this section to assure that handicapped children and their parents or guardians are guaranteed procedural safeguards with respect to the provision of free appropriate public education by such agencies and units.

(b)(1) The procedures required by this section shall include, but shall not be limited to—

(A) an opportunity for the parents or guardian of a handicapped child to examine all relevant records with respect to the identification, evaluation, and educational placement of the child, and the provision of a free appropriate public education to such child, and to obtain an independent educational evaluation of the child;

(B) procedures to protect the rights of the child whenever the parents or guardian of the child are not known, unavailable, or the child is a ward of the State, including the assignment of an individual (who shall not be an employee of the State educational agency, local educational agency, or intermediate educational unit involved in the education or care of the child) to act as a surrogate for the parents or guardian;

(C) written prior notice to the parents or guardian of the child whenever such agency or unit—

(i) proposes to initiate or change, or

(ii) refuses to initiate or change,

the identification, evaluation, or educational placement of the child or the provision of a free appropriate public education to the child;

(D) procedures designed to assure that the notice required by clause (C) fully inform the parents or guardian, in the parents' or guardian's native language, unless it clearly is not feasible to do so, of all procedures available pursuant to this section; and

(E) an opportunity to present complaints with respect to any matter relating to the identification, evaluation, or educational placement of the child, or the provision of a free appropriate public education to such child.

(2) Whenever a complaint has been received under paragraph (1) of this subsection, the parents or guardian shall have an opportunity for an impartial due process hearing which shall be conducted by the State educational agency or by the local educational agency or intermediate educational unit, as determined by State law or by the State educational agency. No hearing conducted pursuant to the requirements of this paragraph shall be conducted by an employee of such

agency or unit involved in the education or care of the child.

(c) If the hearing required in paragraph (2) of subsection (b) of this section is conducted by a local educational agency or an intermediate educational unit, any party aggrieved by the findings and decision rendered in such a hearing may appeal to the State educational agency which shall conduct an impartial review of such hearing. The officer conducting such review shall make an independent decision upon completion of such review.

(d) Any party to any hearing conducted pursuant to subsections (b) and (c) shall be accorded (1) the right to be accompanied and advised by counsel and by individuals with special knowledge or training with respect to the problems of handicapped children, (2) the right to present evidence and confront, cross-examine, and compel the attendance of witnesses, (3) the right to a written or electronic verbatim record of such hearing, and (4) the right to written findings of fact and decisions (which findings and decisions shall also be transmitted to the advisory panel established pursuant to section 613(a)(12)).

(e)(1) A decision made in a hearing conducted pursuant to paragraph (2) of subsection (b) shall be final, except that any party involved in such hearing may appeal such decision under the provisions of subsection (c) and paragraph (2) of this subsection. A decision made under subsection (c) shall be final, except that any party may bring an action under paragraph (2) of this subsection.

(2) Any party aggrieved by the findings and decision made under subsection (b) who does not have the right to an appeal under subsection (c), and any party aggrieved by the findings and decision under subsection (c), shall have the right to bring a civil action with respect to the complaint presented pursuant to this section, which action may be brought in any State court of competent jurisdiction or in a district court of the United States without regard to the amount in controversy. In any action brought under this paragraph the court shall receive the records of the administrative proceedings, shall hear additional evidence at the request of a party, and, basing its decision on the preponderance of the evidence, shall grant such relief as the court determines is appropriate.

(3) During the pendency of any proceedings conducted pursuant to this section, unless the State or local educational agency and the parents or guardian otherwise agree, the child shall remain in the then current educational placement of such child, or, if applying for initial admission to a public school, shall, with the consent of the parents or guardian, be placed in the public school program until all such proceedings have been completed.

(4) The district courts of the United States shall have jurisdiction of actions brought under this subsection without regard to the amount in controversy. *(20 USC 1415)*

WITHHOLDING AND JUDICIAL REVIEW

SEC. 616. (a) Whenever the Secretary, after reasonable notice and

opportunity for hearing to the State educational agency involved (and to any local educational agency or intermediate educational unit affected by any failure described in clause (2)), finds —
    (1) that there has been a failure to comply substantially with any provision of section 612 or section 613, or
    (2) that in the administration of the State plan there is a failure to comply with any provision of this part or with any requirements set forth in the application of a local educational agency or intermediate educational unit approved by the State educational agency pursuant to the State plan,
the Secretary (A) shall, after notifying the State educational agency, withhold any further payments to the State under this part, and (B) may, after notifying the State educational agency, withhold futher payments to the State under the Federal programs specified in section 613(a)(2) within his jurisdiction, to the extent that funds under such programs are available for the provision of assistance for the education of handicapped children. If the Secretary withholds further payments under clause (A) or clause (B) he may determine that such withholding will be limited to programs or projects under the State plan, or portions thereof, affected by the failure, or that the State educational agency shall not make further payments under this part to specified local educational agencies or intermediate educational units affected by the failure. Until the Secretary is satisfied that there is no longer any failure to comply with the provisions of this part, as specified in clause (1) or clause (2), no further payment shall be made to the State under this part or under the Federal programs specified in section 613(a)(2) within his jurisdiction to the extent that funds under such programs are available for the provision of assistance for the education of handicapped children, or payments by the State educational agency under this part shall be limited to local educational agencies and intermediate educational units whose actions did not cause or were not involved in the failure, as the case may be. Any State educational agency, local educational agency, or intermediate educational unit in receipt of a notice pursuant to the first sentence of this subsection shall, by means of a public notice, take such measures as may be necessary to bring the pendency of an action pursuant to this subsection to the attention of the public within the jurisdiction of such agency or unit.

  (b)(1) If any State is dissatisfied with the Secretary's final action with respect to its State plan submitted under section 613, such State may, within sixty days after notice of such action, file with the United States court of appeals for the circuit in which such State is located a petition for review of that action. A copy of the petition shall be forthwith transmitted by the clerk of the court to the Secretary. The Secretary thereupon shall file in the court the record of the proceedings on which he based his action, as provided in section 2112 of title 28, United States Code.

  (2) The findings of fact by the Secretary, if supported by substantial

evidence, shall be conclusive, but the court, for good cause shown, may remand the cause to the Secretary to take further evidence, and the Secretary may thereupon make new or modified findings of fact and may modify his previous action, and shall file in the court the record of the further proceedings. Such new or modified findings of fact shall likewise be conclusive if supported by substantial evidence.

(3) Upon the filing of such petition, the court shall have jurisdiction to affirm the action of the Secretary or to set it aside, in whole or in part. The judgment of the court shall be subject to review by the Supreme Court of the United States upon certiorari or certification as provided in section 1254 of title 28, United States Code. *(20 USC 1416)*

ADMINISTRATION

SEC. 617. (a)(1) In carrying out his duties under this part, the Secretary shall—

(A) cooperate with, and furnish all technical assistance necessary, directly or by grant or contract, to the States in matters relating to the education of handicapped children and the execution of the provisions of this part;

(B) provide such short-term training programs and institutes as are necessary;

(C) disseminate information, and otherwise promote the education of all handicapped children within the States; and

(D) assure that each State shall, within one year after the date of the enactment of the Education for All Handicapped Children Act of 1975, provide certification of the actual number of handicapped children receiving special education and related services in each State.

(2) As soon as practicable after the date of the enactment of the Education for All Handicapped Children Act of 1975, the Secretary shall, by regulation, prescribe a uniform financial report to be utilized by State educational agencies in submitting plans under this part in order to assure equity among the States.

(b) In carrying out the provisions of this part, the Secretary (and the Secretary, in carrying out the provisions of subsection (c)) shall issue, not later than January 1, 1977, amend, and revoke such rules and regulations as may be necessary. No other less formal method of implementing such provisions is authorized.

(c) The Secretary shall take appropriate action, in accordance with the provisions of section 438 of the General Education Provisions Act, to assure the protection of the confidentiality of any personally identifiable data, information, and records collected or maintained by the Secretary and by State and local educational agencies pursuant to the provisions of this part.

(d) The Secretary is authorized to hire qualified personnel necessary to conduct data collection and evaluation activities required by subsections (b), (c) and (d) of section 618 and to carry out his duties under subsection (a)(1) of this subsection without regard to the provisions of title 5, United States Code, relating to appointments in the competitive service and without regard to chapter 51 and subchapter III of chapter 53 of such title relating to classification and general schedule pay rates except that no more than twenty such personnel shall be employed at any time. *(20 USC 1417)*

EVALUATION

SEC. 618. (a) The Secretary shall directly or by grant, contract, or cooperative agreement, collect data and conduct studies, investigations, and evaluations—
    (1) to assess progress in the implementation of this Act, the impact, and the effectiveness of State and local efforts and efforts by the Secretary of Interior to provide free appropriate public education to all handicapped children and youth and early intervention services to handicapped infants and toddlers, and
    (2) to provide—
        (A) Congress with information relevant to policymaking, and
        (B) Federal, State, and local agencies and the Secretary of Interior with information relevant to program management, administration, and effectiveness with respect to such education and early intervention services.

(b) In carrying out subsection (a), the Secretary, on at least an annual basis, shall obtain data concerning programs and projects assisted under this Act and under other Federal laws relating to handicapped infants, toddlers, children, and youth, and such additional information, from State and local educational agencies, the Secretary of Interior, and other appropriate sources, as is necessary for the implementation of this Act including—
    (1) the number of handicapped infants, toddlers, children, and youth in each State receiving a free appropriate public education or early intervention services (A) in age groups 0-2 and 3-5, and (B) in age groups 6-11, 12-17, and 18-21 by disability category,
    (2) the number of handicapped children and youth in each State who are participating in regular educational programs (consistent with the requirements of sections 612(5)(B) and 614(a)(1)(C)(iv) by disability category, and the number of handicapped children and youth in separate classes, separate schools or facilities, or public or private residential facilities or who have been otherwise removed from the regular education environment, *(20 USC 1412, 1414)*
    (3) the number of handicapped children and youth exiting the educational system each year through program completion or otherwise (A) in age group 3-5, and (B) in age groups 6-11,

12-17, and 18-21 by disability category and anticipated services for the next year,

(4) the amount of Federal, State, and local funds expended in each State specifically for special education and related services and for early intervention services (which may be based upon a sampling of data from State agencies including State and local educational agencies),

(5) the number and type of personnel that are employed in the provision of special education and related services to handicapped children and youth and early intervention services to handicapped infants and toddlers by disability category served, and the estimated number and type of additional personnel by disability category needed to adequately carry out the policy established by this Act, and

(6) a description of the special education and related services and early intervention services needed to fully implement this Act throughout each State, including estimates of the number of handicapped infants and toddlers in the 0-2 age group and estimates of the number of handicapped children and youth (A) in age group 3-5 and (B) in age groups 6-11, 12-17, and 18-21 and by disability category.

(c) The Secretary shall, by grant, contract, or cooperative agreement, provide for evaluation studies to determine the impact of this Act. Each such evaluation shall include recommendations for improvement of the programs under this Act. The Secretary shall, not later than July 1 of each year, submit to the appropriate committees of each House of the Congress and publish in the Federal Register proposed evaluation priorities for review and comment.

(d)(1) The Secretary may enter into cooperative agreements with State educational agencies and other State agencies to carry out studies to assess the impact and effectiveness of programs assisted under this Act.

(2) An agreement under paragraph (1) shall —

(A) provide for the payment of not to exceed 60 percent of the total cost of studies conducted by a participating State agency to assess the impact and effectiveness of programs assisted under this Act, and

(B) be developed in consultation with the State Advisory Panel established under this Act, the local educational agencies, and others involved in or concerned with the education of handicapped children and youth and the provision of early intervention services to handicapped infants and toddlers.

(3) The Secretary shall provide technical assistance to participating State agencies in the implementation of the study design, analysis, and reporting procedures.

(4) In addition, the Secretary shall disseminate information from such studies to State agencies, regional resources centers, and clearinghouses established by this Act, and, as appropriate, to others

involved in, or concerned with, the education of handicapped children and youth and the provision of early intervention services to handicapped infants and toddlers.

(e)(1) At least one study shall be a longitudinal study of a sample of handicapped students, encompassing the full range of handicapping conditions, examining their educational progress while in special education and their occupational, educational and independent living status after graduating from secondary school or otherwise leaving special education.

(2) At least one study shall focus on obtaining and compiling current information available, through State educational agencies and local educational agencies and other service providers, regarding State and local expenditures for educational services for handicapped students (including special education and related services) and shall gather information needed in order to calculate a range of per pupil expenditures by handicapping condition.

(f)(1) Not later than 120 days after the close of each fiscal year, the Secretary shall publish and disseminate an annual report on the progress being made toward the provision of a free appropriate public education to all handicapped children and youth and early intervention services for handicapped infants and toddlers. The annual report shall be transmitted to the appropriate committees of each House of Congress and published and disseminated in sufficient quantities to the education community at large and to other interested parties.

(2) The Secretary shall include in each annual report under paragraph (1)—

(A) a compilation and analysis of data gathered under subsection (b)

(B) an index and summary of each evaluation activity and results of studies conducted under subsection (c),

(C) a description of findings and determinations resulting from monitoring reviews of State implementation of part B of this Act, *(20 USC 1411)*

(D) an analysis and evaluation of the participation of handicapped children and youth in vocational education programs and services,

(E) an analysis and evaluation of the effectiveness of procedures undertaken by each State educational agency, local educational agency, and intermediate educational unit to ensure that handicapped children and youth receive special education and related services in the least restrictive environment commensurate with their needs and to improve programs of instruction for handicapped children and youth in day or residential facilities, and

(F) any recommendation for change in the provisions of this Act or any other Federal law providing support for the education of handicapped children and youth.

(3) In the annual report under paragraph (1) for fiscal year 1985 which is published in 1986 and for every third year thereafter, the Secretary shall include in the annual report—
(A) an index of all current projects funded under parts C through G of this title, and *(20 USC 1421-1454)*
(B) data reported under sections 621, 622, 623, 627, 634, 641 and 661. *(20 USC 1421-1454)*

(4) In the annual report under paragraph (1) for fiscal year 1988 which is published in 1989, the Secretary shall include special sections addressing the provision of a free appropriate public education to handicapped infants, toddlers, children, and youth in rural areas and to handicapped migrants, handicapped Indians (particularly programs operated under section 611(f)), handicapped Native Hawaiian, and other native Pacific basin children and youth, handicapped infants, toddlers, children and youth of limited English proficiency. *(20 USC 1426, 1434)*

(5) Beginning in 1986, in consultation with the National Council for the Handicapped and the Bureau of Indian Affairs Advisory Committee for Exceptional Children, a description of the status of early intervention services for handicapped infants and toddlers from birth through age two, inclusive, and special education and related services to handicapped children from 3 through 5 years of age (including those receiving services through Head Start, Developmental Disabilities Programs, Crippled Children's Services, Mental Health/Mental Retardation Agency, and State child-development centers and private agencies under contract with local schools).

(g) There are authorized to be appropriated $3,800,000 for fiscal year 1987, $4,000,000 for fiscal year 1988, and $4,200,000 for fiscal year 1989 to carry out this section.

PRE-SCHOOL GRANTS

SEC. 619. (a)(1) For fiscal years 1987 through 1989 (or fiscal year 1990 if the Secretary makes a grant under this paragraph for such fiscal year) the Secretary shall make a grant to any State which—
(A) has met the eligibility requirements of section 612, *(20 USC 1412)*
(B) has a State plan approved under section 613, and *(20 USC 1413)*
(C) provides special education and related services to handicapped children aged three to five, inclusive.

(2)(A) For fiscal year 1987 the amount of a grant to a State under paragraph (1) may not exceed—
(i) $300 per handicapped child aged three to five, inclusive, who received special education and related services in such State as determined under section 611(a)(3), or *(20 USC 1411)*
(ii) if the amount appropriated under subsection (e) exceeds the product of $300 and the total number of handicapped children aged three to five, inclusive, who received special

education and related services as determined under section 611(a)(3)—
 (I) $300 per handicapped child aged three to five, inclusive, who received special education and related services in such State as determined under section 611(a)(3), plus
 (II) an amount equal to the portion of the appropriation available after allocating funds to all States under subclause (1) (the excess appropriation) divided by the estimated increase, from the preceding fiscal year, in the number of handicapped children aged three to five, inclusive, who will be receiving special education and related services in all States multiplied by the estimated number of such children in such State.
(B) For fiscal year 1988, funds shall be distributed in accordance with clause (i) or (ii) of paragraph (2)(A), except that the amount specified therein shall be $400 instead of $300.
(C) For fiscal year 1989, funds shall be distributed in accordance with clause (i) or (ii) of paragraph (2)(A), except that the amount specified therein shall be $500 instead of $300.
(D) If the Secretary makes a grant under paragraph (1) for fiscal year 1990, the amount of a grant to a State under such paragraph may not exceed $1,000 per handicapped child aged three to five, inclusive, who received special education and related services in such State as determined under section 611(a)(3). *(20 USC 1411)*
(E) If the actual number of additional children served in a fiscal year differs from the estimate made under clause (ii)(II) of the applicable subparagraph, subparagraph (A)(ii)(II), the Secretary shall adjust (upwards or downwards) a State's allotment in the subsequent fiscal year.
(F)(i) The amount of a grant under subparagraph (A), (B), or (C) to any State for a fiscal year may not exceed $3,800 per estimated handicapped child aged three to five, inclusive, who will be receiving or handicapped child aged three to five, inclusive, who is receiving special education and related services in such State.
(ii) If the amount appropriated under subsection (e) for any fiscal year exceeds the amount of grants which may be made to the States for such fiscal year, the excess amount appropriated shall remain available for obligation under this section for 2 succeeding fiscal years.
(3) To receive a grant under paragraph (1) a State shall make an application to the Secretary at such time, in such manner, and containing or accompanied by such information as the Secretary may reasonably require.
(b)(1) For fiscal year 1990 (or fiscal year 1991 if required by paragraph (2)) and fiscal years thereafter the Secretary shall make a grant to any State which—
 (A) has met the eligibility requirements of section 612, and
 (B) has a State plan approved under section 613 which

Education Of The Handicapped Act

includes policies and procedures that assure the availability under the State law and practice of such State of a free appropriate public education for all handicapped children aged three to five, inclusive.

(2) The Secretary may make a grant under paragraph (1) only for fiscal 1990 and fiscal years thereafter, except that if—

(A) the aggregate amount that was appropriated under subsection (e) for fiscal years 1987, 1988, and 1989 was less than $656,000,000, and

(B) the amount appropriated for fiscal year 1990 under subsection (e) is less than $306,000,000,

the Secretary may not make a grant under paragraph (1) until fiscal year 1991 and shall make a grant under subsection (a)(1) for fiscal year 1990.

(3) The amount of any grant to any State under paragraph (1) for any fiscal year may not exceed $1,000 for each handicapped child in such State aged three to five, inclusive.

(4) To receive a grant under paragraph (1) a State shall make an application to the Secretary at such time, in such manner and containing or accompanied by such information as the Secretary may reasonably require.

(c)(1) For fiscal year 1987, a State which receives a grant under subsection (a)(1) shall—

(A) distribute at least 70 percent of such grant to local educational agencies and intermediate educational units in such State in accordance with paragraph (3), except that in applying such section only handicapped children aged three to five, inclusive, shall be considered.

(B) use not more than 25 percent of such grant for the planning and development of a comprehensive delivery system for which a grant could have been made under section 623(b) in effect through fiscal year 1987 and for direct and support services for handicapped children, and

(C) use not more than 5 percent of such grant for administrative expenses related to the grant.

(2) For fiscal years beginning after fiscal year 1987, a State which receives a grant under subsection (a)(1) or (b)(1) shall—

(A) distribute at least 75 percent of such grant to local educational agencies and intermediate educational units in such State in accordance with paragraph (3), except that in applying such section only handicapped children aged three to five, inclusive, shall be considered,

(B) use not more than 20 percent of such grant for the planning and development of a comprehensive delivery system for which a grant could have been made under section 623(b) in effect through fiscal year 1987 and for direct and support services for handicapped children, and

(C) use not more than 5 percent of such grant for administrative expenses related to the grant.

(3) From the amount of funds available to local educational agencies and intermediate educational units in any State under this section, each local educational agency or intermediate educational unit shall be entitled to—

(A) an amount which bears the same ratio to the amount available under subsection (a)(2)(A)(i) or subsection (a)(2)(A)(ii)(I), as the case may be, as the number of handicapped children aged three to five, inclusive, who received special education and related services, as determined under section 611(a)(3) in such local educational agency or intermediate educational unit bears to the aggregate number of handicapped children aged three to five, inclusive, who received special education and related services in all local educational agencies and intermediate educational units in the State entitled to funds under this section, and *(20 USC 1411)*

(B) to the extent funds are available under subsection (a)(2)(A)(ii)(II), an amount which bears the same ratio to the amount available under subsection (a)(2)(A)(ii)(II) as the estimated number of additional handicapped children aged three to five, inclusive, who will be receiving special education and related services in such local educational agency or intermediate educational unit bears to the aggregate number of handicapped children aged three to five, inclusive, who will be receiving special education and related services in all local educational agencies and intermediate educational units in the State entitled to funds under this section.

(d) If the sums appropriated under subsection (e) for any fiscal year for making payments to States under subsection (a)(1) or (b)(1) are not sufficient to pay in full the maximum amounts which all States may receive under such subsection for such fiscal year, the maximum amounts which all States may receive under such subsection for such fiscal year shall be ratably reduced by first ratably reducing amounts computed under the excess appropriation provision of subsection (a)(2)(A)(ii)(II). If additional funds become available for making such payments for any fiscal year during which the preceding sentence is applicable, the reduced maximum amounts shall be increased on the same basis as they were reduced.

(e) For grants under subsections (a)(1) and (b)(1) there are authorized to be appropriated such sums as may be necessary.

PAYMENTS

SEC. 620. (a) The Secretary shall make payments to each State in amounts which the State educational agency of such State is eligible to receive under this part. Any State educational agency receiving payments under this subsection shall distribute payments to the local educational agencies and intermediate educational units of such State in amounts which such agencies and units are eligible to

Education Of The Handicapped Act

receive under this part after the State educational agency has approved applications of such agencies or units for payments in accordance with section 614(b).

(b) Payments under this part may be made in advance or by way of reimbursement and in such installments as the Secretary may determine necessary. *(20 USC 1420)*

PART C—CENTERS AND SERVICES TO MEET SPECIAL NEEDS OF THE HANDICAPPED

REGIONAL RESOURCE AND FEDERAL CENTERS

SEC. 621. (a) The Secretary may make grants to, or enter into contracts or cooperative agreements with, institutions of higher education, public agencies, private nonprofit organizations, State educational agencies, or combinations of such agencies or institutions (which combinations may include one or more local educational agencies) within particular regions of the United States, to pay all or part of the cost of the establishment and operation of regional resource centers. Each regional resource center shall provide consultation, technical assistance, and training to State educational agencies and through such State educational agencies to local educational agencies and to other appropriate State agencies providing early intervention services. The services provided by a regional resource center shall be consistent with the priority needs identified by the States served by the center and the findings of the Secretary in monitoring reports prepared by the Secretary under section 617 of the Act. Each regional resource center established or operated under this section shall— *(20 USC 1417)*

(1) assist in identifying and solving persistent problems in providing quality special education and related services for handicapped children and early intervention services to handicapped infants and toddlers and their families,

(2) assist in developing, identifying, and replicating successful programs and practices which will improve special education and related services to handicapped children and youth and their families and early intervention services to handicapped infants and toddlers and their families,

(3) gather and disseminate information to all State educational agencies within the region and coordinate activities with other centers assisted under this subsection and other relevant projects conducted by the Department of Education,

(4) assist in the improvement of information dissemination to and training activities for professionals and parents of handicapped infants, toddlers, children, and youth, and

(5) provide information to and training for agencies, institutions, and organizations, regarding techniques and approaches for submitting applications for grants, contracts, and cooperative agreements under this part and parts D through G. *(20 USC 1422-1454)*

(b) In determining whether to approve an application for a project under subsection (a), the Secretary shall consider the need for such a center in the region to be served by the applicant and the capability of the applicant to fulfill the responsibilities under subsection (a).

(c) Each regional resource center shall report a summary of materials produced or developed and the summaries reported shall be included in the annual report to Congress required under section 618. *(20 USC 1418)*

(d) The Secretary may establish one coordinating technical assistance center focusing on national priorities established by the Secretary to assist the regional resource centers in the delivery of technical assistance, consistent with such national priorities.

(e) Before using funds made available in any fiscal year to carry out this section for purposes of subsection (d), not less than the amount made available for this section in the previous fiscal year shall be made available for regional resource centers under subsection (a) and in no case shall more than $500,000 be made available for the center under subsection (d). *(20 USC 1421)*

SERVICES FOR DEAF-BLIND CHILDREN AND YOUTH

SEC. 622. (a)(1) The Secretary is authorized to make grants to, or to enter into cooperative agreements or contracts with, public or nonprofit private agencies, institutions, or organizations to assist State edcuational agencies to—

(A) assure deaf-blind children and youth provision of special education and related services as well as vocational and transitional services; and

(B) make available to deaf-blind youth upon attaining the age of twenty-two, programs and services to facilitate their transition from educational to other services; and

(2) A grant, cooperative agreement, or contract pursuant to paragraph (1)(A) may be made only for programs providing (A) technical assistance to agencies, institutions, or organizations providing educational services to deaf-blind children or youth; (B) preservice or inservice training to paraprofessionals, professionals, and related services personnel preparing to serve, or serving, deaf-blind children or youth; (C) replication of successful innovative approaches to providing educational or related services to deaf-blind children and youth; and (D) facilitation of parental involvement in the education of their deaf-blind children and youth. Such programs may include—

(i) the diagnosis and educational evaluation of children and youth at risk of being certified deaf-blind;

(ii) programs of adjustment, education, and orientation for deaf-blind children and youth; and

(iii) consultative, counseling, and training services for the families of deaf-blind children and youth.

(3) A grant, cooperative agreement, or contract pursuant to

paragraph (1)(B) may be made only for programs providing (A) technical assistance to agencies, institutions, and organizations serving, or proposing to serve, deaf-blind individuals who have attained age twenty-two years; (B) training or inservice training to paraprofessionals or professionals serving, or preparing to serve, such individuals; and (C) assistance in the development or replication of successful innovative approaches to providing rehabilitative, semisupervised, or independent living programs.

(4) In carrying out this subsection, the Secretary shall take into consideration the need for a center for deaf-blind children and youth in light of the general availability and quality of existing services for such children and youth in the part of the country involved.

(b) The Secretary is also authorized to enter into a limited number of cooperative agreements or contracts to establish and support regional programs for the provision of technical assistance in the education of deaf-blind children and youth.

(c)(1) Programs supported under this section shall report annually to the Secretary on (A) the numbers of deaf-blind children and youth served by age, severity, and nature of deaf-blindness; (B) the number of paraprofessionals, professionals, and family members directly served by each activity; and (C) the types of services provided.

(2) The Secretary shall examine the number of deaf-blind children and youth (A) reported under subparagraph (c)(1)(A) and by the States; (B) served by the programs under part B of this Act and subpart 2 of part B, title I, of the Elementary and Secondary Education Act of 1965 (as modified by chapter 1 of the Education Consolidation and Improvement Act of 1981); and (C) the Deaf-Blind Registry of each State. The Secretary shall revise the count of deaf-blind children and youth to reflect the most accurate count.

(3) The Secretary shall summarize these data for submission in the annual report required under section 618.

(d) The Secretary shall disseminate materials and information concerning effective practices in working with deaf-blind children and youth.

(e) The Secretary is authorized to make grants to, or enter into contracts or cooperative agreements with, public or nonprofit private agencies, institutions, or organizations for the development and operation of extended school year demonstration programs for severely handicapped children and youth, including deaf-blind children and youth.

(f) The Secretary may make grants to, or enter into contracts or cooperative agreements with, the entities under section 624(a) for the purposes in such section. *(20 USC 1422)*

EARLY EDUCATION FOR HANDICAPPED CHILDREN

SEC. 623. (a)(1) The Secretary may arrange by contract, grant, or cooperative agreement with appropriate public agencies and private nonprofit organizations, for the development and operation of experimental, demonstration, and outreach preschool and early intervention programs for handicapped children which the Secretary determines show promise of promoting a comprehensive and strengthened approach to the special problems of such children. Such programs shall include activities and services designed to (1) facilitate the intellectual, emotional, physical, mental, social, speech, language development, and self-help skills of such children, (2) encourage the participation of the parents of such children in the development and operation of any such program, and (3) acquaint the community to be served by any such program with the problems and potentialities of such children, (4) offer training about exemplary models and practices to State and local personnel who provide services to handicapped children from birth through eight, and (5) support the adaption of exemplary models and practices in States and local communities.

(2) Programs authorized by paragraph (1) shall be coordinated with similar programs in the schools operated or supported by State or local educational agencies of the community to be served and with similar programs operated by other public agencies in such community.

(3) As much as is feasible, programs assisted under paragraph (1) shall be geographically dispersed throughout the Nation in urban as well as rural areas.

(4)(A) Except as provided in subparagraph (B), no arrangement under paragraph (1) shall provide for the payment of more than 90 percent of the total annual costs of development, operation, and evaluation of any program. Non-Federal contributions may be in cash or in kind, fairly evaluated, including plant, equipment, and services.

(B) The Secretary may waive the requirement of subparagraph (A) in the case of an arrangement entered into under paragraph (1) with governing bodies of Indian tribes located on Federal or State reservations and with consortia of such bodies.

(b) The Secretary shall arrange by contract, grant, or cooperative agreement with appropriate public agencies and private nonprofit organizations for the establishment of a technical assistance development system to assist entities operating experimental, demonstration, and outreach programs and to assist State agencies to expand and improve services provided to handicapped children.

(c) The Secretary shall arrange by contract, grant, or cooperative agreement with appropriate public agencies and public nonprofit organizations for the establishment of early childhood research institutes to carry on sustained research to generate and disseminate new information on preschool and early intervention for handicapped children and their families.

(d) The Secretary may make grants to, enter into contracts or cooperative agreements under this section with, such organizations or institutions, as are determined by the Secretary to be appropriate, for research to identify and meet the full range of special needs of handicapped children and for training of personnel for programs specifically designed for handicapped children.

(e) At least one year before the termination of a grant, contract, or cooperative agreement made or entered into under subsections (b) and (c), the Secretary shall publish in the Federal Register a notice of intent to accept application for such a grant, contract, or cooperative agreement contingent on the appropriation of sufficient funds by Congress.

(f) For purposes of this section the term "handicapped children" includes children from birth through eight years of age. *(20 USC 1423)*

PROGRAMS FOR SEVERELY HANDICAPPED CHILDREN

SEC. 624. (a) The Secretary may make grants to, or enter into contracts or cooperative agreements with, such organizations or institutions, as are determined by the Secretary to be appropriate, to address the needs of severely handicapped children and youth, for —

(1) research to identify and meet the full range of special needs of such handicapped children and youth,

(2) the development or demonstration of new, or improvements in, existing, methods, approaches, or techniques which would contribute to the adjustment and education of such handicapped children and youth,

(3) training of personnel for programs specifically designed for such children, and

(4) dissemination of materials and information about practices found effective in working with such children and youth.

(b) In making grants and contracts under subsection (a), the Secretary shall ensure that the activities funded under such grants and contracts will be coordinated with similar activities funded from grants and contracts under other sections of this Act.

(c) To the extent feasible, programs, authorized by subsection (a) shall be geographically dispersed throughout the nation in urban and rural areas. *(20 USC 1424)*

POSTSECONDARY EDUCATION

SEC. 625. (a)(1) The Secretary may make grants to, or enter into contracts with, State educational agencies, institutions of higher education, junior and community colleges, vocational and technical institutions, and other appropriate nonprofit educational agencies for the development, operation, and dissemination of specifically designed model programs of postsecondary, vocational, technical, continuing, or adult education for handicapped individuals.

(2) In making grants or contracts on a competitive basis under paragraph (1), the Secretary shall give priority consideration to 4 regional centers for the deaf and to model programs for individuals with handicapping conditions other than deafness —

(A) for developing and adapting programs of postsecondary, vocational, technical, continuing, or adult education to meet the special needs of handicapped individuals, and

(B) for programs that coordinate, facilitate, and encourage education of handicapped individuals with their nonhandicapped peers.

(3) Persons operating programs for handicapped persons under a grant or contract under paragraph (1) must coordinate their efforts with and disseminate information about their activities to the clearinghouse on postsecondary programs established under section 633(b). *(20 USC 1433)*

(4) At least one year before the termination of a grant or contract with any of the 4 regional centers for the deaf, the Secretary shall publish in the Federal Register a notice of intent to accept application for such grant or contract, contingent on the appropriation of sufficient funds by Congress.

(5) To the extent feasible, programs authorized by paragraph (1) shall be geographically dispensed throughout the nation in urban and rural areas.

(6) Of the sums made available for programs under paragraph (1), not less than $2,000,000 shall first be available for the 4 regional centers for the deaf.

(b) For the purposes of subsection (a) the term "handicapped individuals" means individuals who are mentally retarded, hard of hearing, deaf, speech or language impaired, visually handicapped, seriously emotionally disturbed, orthopedically impaired, other health impaired individuals, or individuals with specific learning disabilities who by reason thereof require special education and related services.

SECONDARY EDUCATION AND TRANSITIONAL SERVICES FOR HANDICAPPED YOUTH

SEC. 626. (a) The Secretary may make grants to, or enter into contracts with, institutions of higher education, State educational agencies, local educational agencies, or other appropriate public and private nonprofit institutions or agencies (including the State job training coordinating councils and service delivery area administrative entities established under the Job Training Partnership Act (Public Law 97-300)) to— *(29 USC 1501 note)*

(1) strengthen and coordinate special education and related services for handicapped youth currently in school or who recently left school to assist them in the transition of postsecondary education, vocational training, competitive employment (including supported employment), continuing education, or adult services,

(2) stimulate the improvements and development of programs for secondary special education, and

(3) stimulate the improvement of the vocational and life

skills of handicapped students to enable them to be better prepared for transition to adult life and services.
To the extent feasible, such programs shall be geographically dispersed through the Nation in urban and rural areas.

(b) Projects assisted under subsection (a) may include —

(1) developing strategies and techniques for transition to independent living, vocational training, vocational rehabilitation, postsecondary education, and competitive employment (including supported employment) for handicapped youth,

(2) establishing demonstration models for services, programs, and individualized education programs, which emphasize vocational training, transitional services, and placement for handicapped youth,

(3) conducting demographic studies which provide information on the numbers, age levels, types of handicapping conditions, and services required for handicapped youth in need of transitional programs,

(4) specially designed vocational programs to increase the potential for competitive employment for handicapped youth,

(5) research and development projects for exemplary service delivery models and the replication and dissemination of successful models,

(6) initiating cooperative models between educational agencies and adult service agencies, including vocational rehabilitation, mental health, mental retardation, public employment, and employers, which facilitate the planning and developing of transitional services for handicapped youth to postsecondary education and vocational training, employment, continuing education, and adult services,

(7) developing appropriate procedures for evaluating vocational training, placement, and transitional services for handicapped youth,

(8) conducting studies which provide information on the numbers, age levels, types of handicapping conditions and reasons why handicapped youth drop out of school,

(9) developing special education curriculum and instructional techniques that will improve handicapped students' acquisition of the skills necessary for transition to adult life and services, and

(10) specifically designed physical education and therapeutic recreation programs to increase the potential of handicapped youths for community participation.

(c) For purposes of paragraphs (1) and (2) of subsection (b), if an applicant is not an educational agency, such applicant shall coordinate with the State educational agency.

(d) Applications for assistance under subsection (a) other than for the purpose of conducting studies or evaluations shall —

(1) describe the procedures to be used for disseminating

relevant findings and data to regional resource centers, clearinghouses, and other interested persons, agencies, or organizations,

(2) describe the procedures that will be used for coordinating services among agencies for which handicapped youth are or will be eligible, and

(3) to the extent appropriate, provide for the direct participation of handicapped students and the parents of handicapped students in the planning, development, and implementation of such projects.

(e) The Secretary is authorized to make grants to, or to enter into contracts or cooperative agreements with, such organizations or institutions as are determined by the Secretary to be appropriate for the development or demonstration of new or improvements in existing methods, approaches, or techniques which will contribute to the adjustment and education of handicapped children and youth and the dissemination of materials and information concerning practices found effective in working with such children and youth.

(f) The Secretary, as appropriate, shall coordinate programs described under subsection (a) with projects developed under section 311 of the Rehabilitation Act of 1973 (29 U.S.C. 777a). *(20 USC 1425)*

PROGRAM EVALUATIONS

SEC. 627. The Secretary shall conduct, either directly or by contract, a thorough and continuing evaluation of the effectiveness of each program assisted under this part. Results of the evaluations shall be analyzed and submitted to the appropriate committees of each House of Congress together with the annual report under section 618. *(20 USC 1426)*

AUTHORIZATION OF APPROPRIATIONS

SEC. 628. (a) There are authorized to be appropriated to carry out section 621, $6,700,000 for fiscal year 1987, $7,100,000 for fiscal year 1988, and $7,500,000 for fiscal year 1989.

(b) There are authorized to be appropriated to carry out section 622, $15,900,000 for fiscal year 1987, $16,800,000 for fiscal year 1988, and $17,800,000 for fiscal year 1989.

(c) There are authorized to be appropriated to carry out section 623, $24,470,000 for fiscal year 1987, $25,870,000 for fiscal year 1988, and $27,410,000 for fiscal year 1989.

(d) There are authorized to be appropriated to carry out section 624, $5,300,000 for fiscal year 1987, $5,600,000 for fiscal year 1988, and $5,900,000 for fiscal year 1989.

(e) There are authorized to be appropriated to carry out section 625, $5,900,000 for fiscal year 1987, $6,200,000 for fiscal year 1988, and $6,600,000 for fiscal year 1989.

(f) There are authorized to be appropriated to carry out section 626, $7,300,000 for fiscal year 1987, $7,700,000 for fiscal year

1988, and $8,100,000 for fiscal year 1989. *(20 USC 1427)*

Part D — Training Personnel for the Education of the Handicapped

GRANTS FOR PERSONNEL TRAINING

Sec. 631. (a)(1) The Secretary may make grants, which may include scholarships with necessary stipends and allowances, to institutions of higher education (including the university-affiliated facilities program under the Rehabilitation Act of 1973 and satellite network of the developmental disabilities program) and other appropriate nonprofit agencies to assist them in training personnel for careers in special education and early intervention, including — *(29 USC 701 note)*

(A) special education teaching, including speech-language pathology and audiology, and adaptive physical education,

(B) related services to handicapped children and youth in educational settings,

(C) special education supervision and administration,

(D) special education research, and

(E) training of special education personnel and other personnel providing special services and pre-school and early intervention services for handicapped children.

(2)(A) In making grants under paragraph (1), the Secretary shall base the determination of such grants on information relating to the present and projected need for the personnel to be trained based on identified State, regional, or national shortages, and the capacity of the institution or agency to train qualified personnel, and other information considered appropriate by the Secretary.

(B) The Secretary shall ensure that grants are only made under paragraph (1) to applicant agencies and institutions that meet State and professionally recognized standards for the preparation of special education and related services personnel unless the grant is for the purpose of assisting the applicant agency or institution to meet such standards.

(3) Grants under paragraph (1) may be used by institutions to assist in covering the cost of courses of training or study for such personnel and for establishing and maintaining fellowships or traineeships with such stipends and allowances as may be determined by the Secretary.

(4) The Secretary in carrying out paragraph (1) may reserve a sum not to exceed 5 percent of the amount available for paragraph (1) in each fiscal year for contracts to prepare personnel in areas where shortages exist when a response to that need has not been adequately addressed by the grant process.

(b) The Secretary may make grants to institutions of higher education and other appropriate nonprofit agencies to conduct special projects to develop and demonstrate new approaches (including the application of new technology) for the preservice training purposes set forth in subsection (a), for regular educators, for the training of teachers to work in community and school settings with handicapped secondary school students, and for the inservice training of special education personnel, including classroom aides, related services personnel, and regular education personnel who serve handicapped children and personnel providing early intervention services.

(c)(1) The Secretary may make grants through a separate competition to private nonprofit organizations for the purpose of providing training and information to parents of handicapped children and persons who work with parents to enable such individuals to participate more effectively with professionals in meeting the educational needs of handicapped children. Such grants shall be designed to meet the unique training and information needs of parents of handicapped children living in the area to be served by the grant, particularly those who are members of groups that have been traditionally underrepresented.

(2) In order to receive a grant under paragraph (1) a private nonprofit organization shall—

(A) be governed by a board of directors on which a majority of the members are parents of handicapped children and which includes members who are professionals in the field of special education and related services who serve handicapped children and youth, or if the nonprofit private organization does not have such a board, such organization shall have a membership which represents the interests of individuals with handicapping conditions, and shall establish a special governing committee on which a majority of the members are parents of handicapped children and which includes members who are professionals in the fields of special education and related services to operate the training and information program under paragraph (1).

(B) serve the parents of children with the full range of handicapping conditions under such grant program, and

(C) demonstrate the capacity and expertise to conduct effectively the training and information activities for which a grant may be made under paragraph (1).

(3) The board of directors or special governing committee of a private nonprofit organization receiving a grant under paragraph (1) shall meet at least once in each calendar quarter to review the parent training and information activities for which the grant is made, and each such committee shall advise the governing board directly of its views and recommendations. Whenever a private nonprofit organization requests the renewal of a grant under paragraph (1) for a fiscal year, the board of directors or the special governing committee shall submit to the Secretary a written review of the parent training and information program conducted by that private nonprofit organization during the preceding fiscal year.

(4) The Secretary shall ensure that grants under paragraph (1) will—

(A) be distributed geographically to the greatest extent possible throughout all the States and give priority to grants which involve unserved areas, and

(B) be targeted to parents of handicapped children in both urban and rural areas or on a State or regional basis.

(5) Parent training and information programs assisted under paragraph (1) shall assist parents to—

(A) better understand the nature and needs of the handicapping conditions of children,

(B) provide followup support for handicapped children's educational programs,

(C) communicate more effectively with special and regular educators, administrators, related services personnel, and other relevant professionals,

(D) participate in educational decisionmaking processes including the development of a handicapped child's individualized educational program,

(E) obtain information about the programs, services, and resources available to handicapped children and the degree to which the programs, services, and resources are appropriate, and

(F) understand the provisions for the education of handicapped children as specified under part B of this Act. *(20 USC 1411)*

(6) Parent training and information programs may, at a grant recipient's discretion, include State or local educational personnel where such participation will further an objective of the program assisted by the grant.

(7) Each private nonprofit organization operating a program receiving a grant under paragraph (1) shall consult with appropriate agencies which serve or assist handicapped children and youth and are located in the jurisdictions served by the program.

(8) The Secretary shall provide technical assistance, by grant or contract, for establishing, developing, and coordinating parent training and information programs.

GRANTS TO STATE EDUCATIONAL AGENCIES AND INSTITUTIONS FOR TRAINEESHIPS

SEC. 632. The Secretary shall make grants to each State educational agency and may make grants to institutions of higher education to assist in establishing and maintaining preservice and inservice programs to prepare personnel to meet the needs of handicapped infants, toddlers, children, and youth or supervisors of such persons, consistent with the personnel needs identified in the State's comprehensive system of personnel development under section 613. *(20 USC 1432)*

CLEARINGHOUSES

SEC. 633. (a) The Secretary is authorized to make a grant to or enter into a contract with a public agency or a nonprofit private organization or institution for a national clearinghouse on the education of the handicapped and to make grants or contracts with a public agency or a nonprofit private organization or institution for other support projects which may be deemed necessary by the Secretary to disseminate information and provide technical assistance on a national basis to parents, professionals, and other interested parties concerning —

(1) programs relating to the education of the handicapped under this Act and under other Federal laws, and

(2) participation in such programs, including referral of individuals to appropriate national, State, and local agencies and organizations for further assistance.

(b) In addition to the clearinghouse established under subsection (a), the Secretary shall make a grant or enter into a contract for a national clearinghouse on postsecondary education for handicapped individuals for the purpose of providing information on available services and programs in postsecondary education for the handicapped.

(c) The Secretary shall make a grant or enter into a contract for a national clearinghouse designed to encourage students to seek careers and professional personnel to seek employment in the various fields relating to the education of handicapped children and youth through the following:

(1) Collection and dissemination of information on current and future national, regional, and State needs for special education and related services personnel.

(2) Dissemination to high school counselors and others concerning current career opportunities in special education, location of programs, and various forms of financial assistance (such as scholarships, stipends, and allowances).

(3) Identification of training programs available around the country.

(4) Establishment of a network among local and State educational agencies and institutions of higher education concerning the supply of graduates and available openings.

(5) Technical assistance to institutions seeking to meet State and professionally recognized standards. *(20 USC 1433)*

(d)(1) In awarding the grants and contracts under this section, the Secretary shall give particular attention to any demonstrated experience at the national level relevant to performance of the functions established in the section, and ability to conduct such projects, communicate with the intended consumers of information, and maintain the necessary communication with other agencies and organizations.

(2) The Secretary is authorized to make contracts with profit-making organizations under this section only when necessary for materials or media access. *(20 USC 1433)*

Education Of The Handicapped Act

REPORTS TO THE SECRETARY

SEC. 634. (a) Not more than sixty days after the end of any fiscal year, each recipient of a grant or contract under this part during such fiscal year shall prepare and submit a report to the Secretary. Each such report shall be in such form and detail as the Secretary determines to be appropriate, and shall include —

(1) the number of individuals trained under the grant or contract, by category of training and level of training; and

(2) the number of individuals trained under the grant or contract receiving degrees and certification, by category and level of training.

(b) A summary of the date required by this section shall be included in the annual report of the Secretary under section 618 of this Act. *(20 USC 1434)*

AUTHORIZATION OF APPROPRIATIONS

SEC. 635. (a) There are authorized to be appropriated to carry out this part (other than section 633) $70,400,000 for fiscal year 1987, $74,500,000 for fiscal year 1988, and $79,000,000 for fiscal year 1989. There are authorized to be appropriated to carry out section 633, $1,200,000 for fiscal year 1987, $1,900,000 for fiscal year 1988, and $2,000,000 for fiscal year 1989.

(b) Of the funds appropriated pursuant to subsection (a) for any fiscal year, the Secretary shall reserve not less than 65 per centum for activities described in subparagraphs (A) through (E) of section 631(a)(1).

(c) Of the funds appropriated under subsection (a) for any fiscal year, the Secretary shall reserve 10 percent for activities under section 631(c).

PART E — RESEARCH IN THE EDUCATION OF THE HANDICAPPED

RESEARCH AND DEMONSTRATION PROJECTS IN EDUCATION OF HANDICAPPED CHILDREN

SEC. 641 (a) The Secretary may make grants to, or enter into contracts or cooperative agreements with, State and local educational agencies, institutions of higher education, and other public agencies and nonprofit private organizations for research and related activities to assist special education personnel, related services personnel, early intervention personnel, and other appropriate persons, including parents, in improving the special education and related services and early intervention services for handicapped infants, toddlers, children, and youth. Research and related activities shall be designed to increase knowledge and understanding of handicapping conditions, and teaching, learning, and education-related developmental practices and services for handicapped infants, toddlers, children and youth. Research and related activities assisted under

this section shall include the following:
  (1) The development of new and improved techniques and devices for teaching handicapped infants, toddlers, children and youth.
  (2) The development of curricula which meet the unique educational and developmental needs for handicapped infants, toddlers, children and youth.
  (3) The application of new technologies and knowledge for the purpose of improving the instruction of handicapped infants, toddlers, children and youth.
  (4) The development of program models and exemplary practices areas of special education and early intervention.
  (5) The dissemination of information on research and related activities conducted under this part to regional resource centers and interested individuals and organizations.
  (6) The development of instruments, including tests, inventories, and scales for measuring progress of handicapped infants, toddlers, children and youth across a number of developmental domains.
 (b) In carrying out subsection (a), the Secretary shall consider the special education or early intervention experience of applicants under such subsection.
 (c) The Secretary shall publish proposed research priorities in the Federal Register every 2 years, not later than July 1, and shall allow a period of 60 days for public comments and suggestions. After analyzing and considering the public comments, the Secretary shall publish final research priorities in the Federal Register not later than 30 days after the close of the comment period.
 (d) The Secretary shall provide an index (including the title of each research project and the name and address of the researching organization) of all research projects conducted in the prior fiscal year in the annual report described under section 618. The Secretary shall make reports of research projects available to the education community at large and to other interested parties.
 (e) The Secretary shall coordinate the research priorities established under subsection (c) with research priorities established by the National Institute of Handicapped Research and shall provide information concerning research priorities established under such subsection to the National Council on the Handicapped, and to the Bureau of Indian Affairs Advisory Committee for Exceptional Children. *(20 USC 1441)*

RESEARCH AND DEMONSTRATION PROJECTS IN PHYSICAL
EDUCATION AND RECREATION FOR HANDICAPPED CHILDREN

  SEC. 642. The Secretary is authorized to make grants to States, State or local educational agencies, institutions of higher education, and other public or nonprofit private educational or research agencies and organizations, and to make contracts with States, State or local educational agencies, institutions of higher education, and other public or private educational or research, agencies and organizations, for research and related purposes relating to physical education or recreation for handicapped children, and to conduct research, surveys, or demonstrations relating to physical education or recreation for handicapped children. *(20 USC 1442)*

PANELS OF EXPERTS

SEC. 643. (a) The Secretary shall convene, in accordance with subsection (b), panels of experts who are competent to evaluate proposals for projects under parts C through G. The panels shall be composed of — *(20 USC 1421-1454)*

(1) individuals from the field of special education for the handicapped and other relevant disciplines who have significant expertise and experience in the content areas and age levels addressed in the proposals, and

(2) handicapped individuals and parents of handicapped individuals when appropriate.

(b)(1) The Secretary shall convene panels under subsection (a) for any application which includes a total funding request exceeding $60,000 and may convene or otherwise appoint panels for applications which include funding requests that are less than such amount.

(2) Such panels shall include a majority of non-Federal members. Such non-Federal members shall be provided travel and per diem not to exceed the rate provided to other educational consultants used by the Department and shall be provided consultant fees at such a rate.

(c) The Secretary may use funds available under parts C through G to pay expenses and fees of non-Federal members under subsection (b). *(20 USC 1421-1454)*

AUTHORIZATION OF APPROPRIATIONS

SEC. 644. For purposes of carrying out this part, there are authorized to be appropriated $18,000,000 for fiscal year 1987, $19,000,000 for fiscal year 1988, and $20,100,000 for fiscal year 1989. *(20 USC 1444)*

PART F — INSTRUCTIONAL MEDIA FOR THE HANDICAPPED

PURPOSE

SEC. 651. (a) The purposes of this part are to promote —

(1) the general welfare of deaf persons by (A) bringing to such persons understanding and appreciation of those films which play such an important part in the general and cultural advancement of hearing persons, (B) providing through these films enriched educational and cultural experiences through which deaf persons can be brought into better touch with the

realities of their environment, and (C) providing a wholesome and rewarding experience which deaf persons may share together; and

(2) the educational advancement of handicapped persons by (A) carrying on research in the use of educational media for the handicapped, (B) producing and distributing educational media for the use of handicapped persons, their parents, their actual or potential employers, and other persons directly involved in work for the advancement of the handicapped, and (C) training persons in the use of educational media for the instruction of the handicapped. *(20 USC 1451)*

CAPTIONED FILMS AND EDUCATIONAL MEDIA FOR HANDICAPPED PERSONS

SEC. 652. (a) The Secretary shall establish a loan service of captioned films and educational media for the purpose of making such materials available, in accordance with regulations, in the United States for nonprofit purposes to handicapped persons, parents of handicapped persons, and other persons directly involved in activities for the advancement of the handicapped, including for the purpose of addressing problems of illiteracy among the handicapped.

(b) The Secretary is authorized to—

(1) acquire films (or rights thereto) and other educational media by purchase, lease, or gift;

(2) acquire by lease or purchase equipment necessary to the administration of this part;

(3) provide by grant or contract, for the captioning of films;

(4) provide, by grant or contract, for the distribution of captioned films and other educational media and equipment through State schools for the handicapped, public libraries, and such other agencies as the Secretary may deem appropriate to serve as local or regional centers for such distribution;

(5) provide, by grant or contract, for the conduct of research in the use of educational and training films and other educational media for the handicapped, for the production and distribution of educational and training films and other educational media for the handicapped and the training of persons in the use of such films and media, including the payment to those persons of such stipends (including allowances for travel and other expenses of such persons and their dependents) as he may determine, which shall be consistent with prevailing practices under comparable federally supported programs;

(6) utilize the facilities and services of other governmental agencies; and

(7) accept gifts, contributions, and voluntary and uncompensated services of individuals and organizations; and

(8) provide by grant or contract for educational media and materials for the deaf.

Education Of The Handicapped Act

(c) The Secretary may make grants to or enter into contracts or cooperative agreements with the national Theatre of the Deaf, Inc. for the purpose of providing theatrical experiences to —
    (1) enrich the lives of deaf children and adults,
    (2) increase public awareness and understanding of deafness and of the artistic and intellectual achievements of deaf people, and
    (3) promote the integration of hearing and deaf people through shared cultural experiences. *(20 USC 1452)*

AUTHORIZATION

SEC. 653. For the purposes of carrying out this part, there are authorized to be appropriated $15,000,000 for fiscal year 1987, $15,750,000 for fiscal year 1988, and $16,540,000 for fiscal year 1989. *(20 USC 1454)*

PART G — TECHNOLOGY, EDUCATIONAL MEDIA AND MATERIALS FOR THE HANDICAPPED

FINANCIAL ASSISTANCE

SEC. 661. The Secretary may make grants or enter into contracts or cooperative agreements with institutions of higher education, State and local educational agencies, or other appropriate agencies and organizations for the purpose of advancing the use of new technology, media, and materials in the education of handicapped students and the provision of early intervention to handicapped infants and toddlers. In carrying out this subsection, the Secretary may fund projects or centers for the purposes of — *(20 USC 1461)*
    (1) determining how technology, media, and materials are being used in the education of the handicapped and how they can be used more effectively,
    (2) designing and adapting new technology, media, and materials to improve the education of handicapped students,
    (3) assisting the public and private sectors in the development and marketing of new technology, media, and materials for the education of the handicapped, and
    (4) disseminating information on the availability and use of new technology, media, and materials for the education of the handicapped.

AUTHORIZATION OF APPROPRIATIONS

SEC. 662. For the purposes of carrying out this part, there are authorized to be appropriated $10,000,000 for fiscal year 1987, $10,500,000 for fiscal year 1988, and $11,025,000 for fiscal year 1989. *(20 USC 1462)*

Part H—Handicapped Infants and Toddlers

FINDINGS AND POLICY

SEC. 671. (a) FINDINGS. — The Congress finds that there is an urgent and substantial need — *(20 USC 1471)*

(1) to enhance the development of handicapped infants and toddlers and to minimize their potential for developmental delay,

(2) to reduce the educational costs to our society, including our Nation's schools, by minimizing the need for special education and related services after handicapped infants and toddlers reach school age,

(3) to minimize the likelihood of institutionalization of handicapped individuals and maximize the potential for their independent living in society, and

(4) to enhance the capacity of families to meet the special needs of their infants and toddlers with handicaps.

(b) POLICY. — It is therefore the policy of the United States to provide financial assistance to States —

(1) to develop and implement a statewide, comprehensive, coordinated, multidisciplinary, interagency program of early intervention services for handicapped infants and toddlers and their families,

(2) to facilitate the coordination of payment for early intervention services from Federal, State, local, and private sources (including public and private insurance coverage), and

(3) to enhance its capacity to provide quality early intervention services and expand and improve existing early intervention services being provided to handicapped infants, toddlers, and their families.

DEFINITIONS

SEC. 672. As used in this part — *(20 USC 1472)*

(1) The term "handicapped infants and toddlers" means individuals from birth to age 2, inclusive, who need early intervention services because they —

(A) are experiencing developmental delays, as measured by appropriate diagnostic instruments and procedures in one or more of the following areas: Cognitive development, physical development, language and speech development, psychosocial development, or self-help skills, or

(B) have a diagnosed physical or mental condition which has a high probability of resulting in developmental delay. Such term may also include, at a State's discretion, individuals from birth to age 2, inclusive, who are at risk of having substantial developmental delays if early intervention services are not provided.

(2) "Early intervention services" are developmental services which —

(A) are provided under public supervision,

(B) are provided at no cost except where Federal or State law provides for a system of payments by families, including a schedule of sliding fees,

(C) are designed to meet a handicapped infant's or toddler's developmental needs in any one or more of the following areas:
    (i) physical development,
    (ii) cognitive development,
    (iii) language and speech development,
    (iv) psycho-social development, or
    (v) self-help skills,

(D) meet the standards of the State, including the requirements of this part,

(E) include—
    (i) family training, counseling, and home visits,
    (ii) special instruction,
    (iii) speech pathology and audiology,
    (iv) occupational therapy,
    (v) physical therapy,
    (vi) psychological services,
    (vii) case management services,
    (viii) medical services only for diagnostic or evaluation purposes,
    (ix) early identification, screening, and assessment services, and
    (x) health services necessary to enable the infant or toddler to benefit from the other early intervention services,

(F) are provided by qualified personnel, including—
    (i) special educators,
    (ii) speech and language pathologists and audiologists,
    (iii) occupational therapists,
    (iv) physical therapists,
    (v) psychologists,
    (vi) social workers,
    (vii) nurses, and
    (viii) nutritionists, and

(G) are provided in conformity with an individualized family service plan adopted in accordance with section 677.

(3) The term "developmental delay" has the meaning given such term by a State under section 676(b)(1).

(4) The term "Council" means the State Interagency Coordinating Council established under section 682.

GENERAL AUTHORITY

SEC. 673. The Secretary shall, in accordance with this part, make grants to States (from their allocations under section 684) to assist each State to develop a statewide, comprehensive, coordinated, multidisciplinary, interagency system to provide early intervention services for handicapped infants and toddlers and their families. *(20 USC 1473)*

GENERAL ELIGIBILITY

SEC. 674. In order to be eligible for a grant under section 673 for any fiscal year, a State shall demonstrate to the Secretary (in its application under section 678) that the State has established a State Interagency Coordinating Council which meets the requirements of section 682. *(20 USC 1474)*

CONTINUING ELIGIBILITY

SEC. 675. (a) FIRST TWO YEARS. — In order to be eligible for a grant under section 673 for the first or second year of a State's participation under this part, a State shall include in its application under section 678 for that year assurances that funds received under section 673 shall be used to assist the State to plan, develop, and implement the statewide system required by section 676. *(20 USC 1475)*

(b) THIRD AND FOURTH YEAR. — (1) In order to be eligible for a grant under section 673 for the third or fourth year of a State's participation under this part, a State shall include in its application under Section 678 for that year information and assurances demonstrating to the satisfaction of the Secretary that —

(A) the State has adopted a policy which incorporates all of the components of a statewide system in accordance with section 676 or obtained a waiver from the Secretary under paragraph (2),

(B) funds shall be used to plan, develop, and implement the statewide system required by section 676, and

(C) such statewide system will be in effect no later than the beginning of the fourth year of the State's participation under section 673, except that with respect to section 676(b)(4), a State need only conduct multidisciplinary assessments, develop individualized family service plans, and make available case management services.

(2) Notwithstanding paragraph (1), the Secretary may permit a State to continue to receive assistance under section 673 during such third year even if the State has not adopted the policy required by paragraph (1)(A) before receiving assistance if the State demonstrates in its application —

(A) that the State has made a good faith effort to adopt such a policy,

(B) the reasons why it was unable to meet the timeline and the steps remaining before such a policy will be adopted, and

(C) an assurance that the policy will be adopted and go into effect before the fourth year of such assistance.

(c) FIFTH AND SUCCEEDING YEARS. — In order to be eligible for a grant under section 673 for a fifth and any succeeding year of a State's participation under this part, a State shall include in its application under section 678 for that year information and assurances demonstrating to the satisfaction of the Secretary that the State has in effect the statewide system required by section 676 and a description of services to be provided under section 676(b)(2).

(d) EXCEPTION. — Notwithstanding subsections (a) and (b), a State which has in effect a State law, enacted before September 1, 1986, that requires the provision of free appropriate public education to handicapped children from birth through age 2, inclusive, shall be eligible for a grant under section 673 for the first through fourth years of a State's participation under this part.

REQUIREMENTS FOR STATEWIDE SYSTEM

SEC. 676. (a) IN GENERAL. — A statewide system of coordinated, comprehensive, multidisciplinary, interagency programs providing appropriate early intervention services to all handicapped infants and toddlers and their families shall include the minimum components under subsection (b). *(20 USC 1476)*

(b) MINIMUM COMPONENTS. — The statewide system required by subsection (a) shall include, at a minimum —

(1) a definition of the term "developmentally delayed" that will be used by the State in carrying out programs under this part,

(2) timetables for ensuring that appropriate early intervention services will be available to all handicapped infants and toddlers in the State before the beginning of the fifth year of a State's participation under this part,

(3) a timely, comprehensive, multidisciplinary evaluation of the functioning of each handicapped infant and toddler in the State and the needs of the families to appropriately assist in the development of the handicapped infant or toddler,

(4) for each handicapped infant and toddler in the State, an individualized family service plan in accordance with section 677, including case management services in accordance with such service plan,

(5) a comprehensive child find system, consistent with part B, including a system for making referrals to service providers that includes timelines and provides for the participation by primary referral sources,

(6) a public awareness program focusing on early identification of handicapped infants and toddlers,

(7) a central directory which includes early intervention services, resources, and experts available in the State and research and demonstration projects being conducted in the State,

(8) a comprehensive system of personnel development,

(9) a single line of responsibility in a lead agency designated or established by the Governor for carrying out—

(A) the general administration, supervision, and monitoring of programs and activities receiving assistance under section 673 to ensure compliance with this part,

(B) the identification and coordination of all available resources within the State from Federal, State, local and private sources,

(C) the assignment of financial responsibility to the appropriate agency,

(D) the development of procedures to ensure that services are provided to handicapped infants and toddlers and their families in a timely manner pending the resolution of any disputes among public agencies or service providers,

(E) the resolution of intra- and interagency disputes, and

(F) the entry into formal interagency agreements that define the financial responsibility of each agency for paying for early intervention services (consistent with State law) and procedures for resolving disputes and that include all additional components necessary to ensure meaningful cooperation and coordination,

(10) a policy pertaining to the contracting or making of other arrangements with service providers to provide early intervention services in the State, consistent with the provisions of this part, including the contents of the application used and the conditions of the contract or other arrangements,

(11) a procedure for securing timely reimbursement of funds used under this part in accordance with section 681(a),

(12) procedural safeguards with respect to programs under this part as required by section 680, and

(13) policies and procedures relating to the establishment and maintenance of standards to ensure that personnel necessary to carry out this part are appropriately and adequately prepared and trained, including—

(A) the establishment and maintenance of standards which are consistent with any State approved or recognized certification, licensing, registration, or other comparable requirements which apply to the area in which such personnel are providing early intervention services, and

(B) to the extent such standards are not based on the highest requirements in the State applicable to a specific profession or discipline, the steps the State is taking to require the retraining or hiring of personnel that meet appropriate professional requirements in the State, and

(14) a system for compiling data on the numbers of handicapped infants and toddlers and their families in the State in need of appropriate early intervention services (which may be based on a sampling of data), the numbers of such infants and

toddlers and their families served, the types of services provided (which may be based on a sampling of data), and other information required by the Secretary.

INDIVIDUALIZED FAMILY SERVICE PLAN

SEC. 677. (a) ASSESSMENT AND PROGRAM DEVELOPMENT. — Each handicapped infant or toddler and the infant or toddler's family will receive — *(20 USC 1477)*
 (1) a multidisciplinary assessment to unique needs and the identification of services appropriate to meet such needs, and
 (2) a written individualized family service plan developed by a multidisciplinary team, including the parent or guardian, as required by subsection (d).

(b) PERIODIC REVIEW. — The individualized family service plan shall be evaluated once a year and the family shall be provided a review of the plan at 6 month-intervals (or more often where appropriate based on infant and toddler and family needs).

(c) PROMPTNESS AFTER ASSESSMENT. — The individualized family service plan shall be developed within a reasonable time after the assessment required by subsection (a)(1) is completed. With the parent's consent, early intervention services may commence prior to the completion of such assessment.

(d) CONTENT OF PLAN. — The individualized family service plan shall be in writing and contain —
 (1) a statement of the infant's or toddler's present levels of physical development, cognitive development, language and speech development, psycho-social development, and self-help skills, based on acceptable objective criteria,
 (2) a statement of the family's strengths and needs relating to enhancing the development of the family's handicapped infant or toddler,
 (3) a statement of the major outcomes expected to be achieved for the infant and toddler and the family, and the criteria, procedures, and timelines used to determine the degree to which progress toward achieving the outcomes are being made and whether modifications or revisions of the outcomes or services are necessary,
 (4) a statement of specific early intervention services necessary to meet the unique needs of the infant or toddler and the family, including the frequency, intensity, and the method of delivering services,
 (5) the projected dates for initiation of services and the anticipated duration of such services,
 (6) the name of the case manager from the profession most immediately relevant to the infant's and toddler's or family's needs who will be responsible for the implementation of the plan and coordination with other agencies and persons, and
 (7) the steps to be taken supporting the transition of the

handicapped toddler to services provided under part B to the extent such services are considered appropriate. *(20 USC 1411)*

STATE APPLICATION AND ASSURANCES

SEC. 678. (a) APPLICATION. — Any State desiring to receive a grant under section 673 for any year shall submit an application to the Secretary at such time and in such manner as the Secretary may reasonably require by regulation. Such an application shall contain — *(20 USC 1478)*

    (1) a designation of the lead agency in the State that will be responsible for the administration of funds provided under section 673,

    (2) information demonstrating eligibility of the State under section 674,

    (3) the information or assurances required to demonstrate eligibility of the State for the particular year of participation under section 675, and

    (4)(A) information demonstrating that the State has provided (i) public hearings, (ii) adequate notice of such hearings, and (iii) an opportunity for comment to the general public before the submission of such application and before the adoption by the State of the policies described in such application, and (B) a summary of the public comments and the State's responses,

    (5) a description of the uses for which funds will be expended in accordance with this part and for the fifth and succeeding fiscal years a description of the services to be provided,

    (6) a description of the procedure used to ensure an equitable distribution of resources made available under this part among all geographic areas within the State, and

    (7) such other information and assurances as the Secretary may reasonably require by regulation.

(b) STATEMENT OF ASSURANCES. — Any State desiring to receive a grant under section 673 shall file with the Secretary a statement at such time and in such manner as the Secretary may reasonably require by regulation. Such statement shall —

    (1) assure that funds paid to the State under section 673 will be expended in accordance with this part,

    (2) contain assurances that the State will comply with the requirements of section 681,

    (3) provide satisfactory assurance that the control of funds provided under section 673, and title to property derived therefrom, shall be in a public agency for the uses and purposes provided in this part and that a public agency will administer such funds and property.

    (4) provide for (A) making such reports in such form and containing such information as the Secretary may require to carry out the Secretary's functions under this part, and (B) keeping such records and affording such access thereto as the

Secretary may find necessary to assure the correctness and verification of such reports and proper disbursement of Federal funds under this part,

(5) provide satisfactory assurance that Federal funds made available under section 673 (A) will not be commingled with State funds, and (B) will be so used as to supplement and increase the level of State and local funds expended for handicapped infants and toddlers and their families and in no case to supplant such State and local funds,

(6) provide satisfactory assurance that such fiscal control and fund accounting procedures will be adopted as may be necessary to assure proper disbursement of, and accounting for, Federal funds paid under section 673 to the State, and

(7) such other information and assurances as the Secretary may reasonably require by regulation.

(c) APPROVAL OF APPLICATION AND ASSURANCES REQUIRED. — No state may receive a grant under section 673 unless the Secretary has approved the application and statement of assurances of that state. The Secretary shall not disapprove such an application or statement of assurances unless the Secretary determines, after notice and opportunity for a hearing, that the application or statement of assurances fails to comply with the requirements of this section.

USES OF FUNDS

SEC. 679. In addition to using funds provided under section 673 to plan, develop, and implement the statewide system required by section 676, a State may use such funds — *(20 USC 1479)*

(1) for direct services for handicapped infants and toddlers that are not otherwise provided from other public or private sources, and

(2) to expand and improve on services for handicapped infants and toddlers that are otherwise available.

PROCEDURAL SAFEGUARDS

SEC. 680. The procedural safeguards required to be included in a statewide system under section 676(b)(12) shall provide, at a minimum, the following: *(20 USC 1480)*

(1) The timely administrative resolution of complaints by parents. Any party aggrieved by the findings and decision regarding an administrative complaint shall have the right to bring a civil action with respect to the complaint, which action may be brought in any State court of competent jurisdiction or in a district court of the United States without regard to the amount in controversy. In any action brought under this paragraph, the court shall receive the records of the administrative proceedings, shall hear additional evidence at the request of a party, and, basing its decision on the preponderance of the evidence, shall grant such relief as the court determines is appropriate.

(2) The right to confidentiality of personally identifiable information.

(3) The opportunity for parents and a guardian to examine records relating to assessment, screening, eligibility determinations, and the development and implementation of the individualized family service plan.

(4) Procedures to protect the rights of the handicapped infant and toddlers whenever the parents or guardian of the child are not known or unavailable or the child is a ward of the State, including the assignment of an individual (who shall not be an employee of the State agency providing services) to act as a surrogate for the parents or guardian.

(5) Written prior notice to the parents or guardian of the handicapped infant or toddler whenever the State agency or service provider proposes to initiate or change or refuses to initiate or change the identification, evaluation, placement, or the provision of appropriate early intervention services to the handicapped infant or toddler.

(6) Procedures designed to assure that the notice required by paragraph (5) fully informs the parents or guardian, in the parents' or guardian's native language, unless it clearly is not feasible to do so, of all procedures available pursuant to this section.

(7) During the pendency of any proceeding or action involving a complaint, unless the State agency and the parents or guardian otherwise agree, the child shall continue to receive the appropriate early intervention services currently being provided or if applying for initial services shall receive the services not in dispute.

PAYOR OF LAST RESORT

SEC. 681. (a) NONSUBSTITUTION. — Funds provided under section 673 may not be used to satisfy a financial commitment for services which would have been paid for from another public or private source but for the enactment of this part, except that whenever considered necessary to prevent the delay in the receipt of appropriate early intervention services by the infant or toddler or family in a timely fashion, funds provided under section 673 may be used to pay the provider of services pending reimbursement from the agency which has ultimate responsibility for the payment. *(20 USC 1481)*

(b) REDUCTION OF OTHER BENEFITS. — Nothing in this part shall be construed to permit the State to reduce medical or other assistance available or to alter eligibility under title V of the Social Security Act (relating to maternal and child health) or title XIX of the Social Security Act (relating to medicaid for handicapped infants and toddlers) within the State. *(42 USC 701, 42 USC 1396)*

STATE INTERAGENCY COORDINATING COUNCIL

SEC. 682. (a) ESTABLISHMENT. — (1) Any State which desires to

receive financial assistance under section 673 shall establish a State Interagency Coordinating Council composed of 15 members.
(20 USC 1482)

(2) The council and the chairperson of the Council shall be appointed by the Governor. In making appointments to the Council, the Governor shall ensure that the membership of the Council reasonably represents the population of the State.

(b) COMPOSITION. — The council shall be composed of —

(1) at least 3 parents of handicapped infants or toddlers or handicapped children aged 3 through 6, inclusive,

(2) at least 3 public or private providers of early intervention services,

(3) at least one representative from the State legislature,

(4) at least one person involved in personnel preparation, and

(5) other members representing each of the appropriate agencies involved in the provision of or payment for early intervention services to handicapped infants and toddlers and their families and others selected by the Governor.

(c) MEETINGS. — The Council shall meet at least quarterly and in such places as it deems necessary. The meetings shall be publicly announced, and, to the extent appropriate, open and accessible to the general public.

(d) MANAGEMENT AUTHORITY. — Subject to the approval of the Governor, the Council may prepare and approve a budget using funds under this part to hire staff, and obtain the services of such professional, technical, and clerical personnel as may be necessary to carry out its functions under this part.

(e) FUNCTIONS OF COUNCIL. — The Council shall —

(1) advise and assist the lead agency designated or established under section 676(b)(9) in the performance of the responsibilities set out in such section, particularly the identification of the sources of fiscal and other support for services for early intervention programs, assignment of financial responsibility to the appropriate agency, and the promotion of the interagency agreements,

(2) advise and assist the lead agency in the preparation of applications and amendments thereto, and

(3) prepare and submit an annual report to the Governor and to the Secretary on the status of early intervention programs for handicapped infants and toddlers and their families operated within the State.

(f) CONFLICT OF INTEREST. — No member of the Council shall cast a vote on any matter which would provide direct financial benefit to that member or otherwise give the appearance of a conflict of interest under State law.

(g) USE OF EXISTING COUNCILS. — To the extent that a State has established a Council before September 1, 1986, that is comparable to the Council described in this section, such Council shall be considered to be in compliance with this section. Within 4 years after the date the State accepts funds under section 673, such State shall establish a council that complies in full with this section.

FEDERAL ADMINISTRATION

SEC. 683. Sections 616, 617 and 620 shall, to the extent not inconsistent with this part, apply to the program authorized by this part, except that—*(20 USC 1483)*

(1) any reference to a State educational agency shall be deemed to be a reference to the State agency established or designated under section 676(b)(9), *(20 USC 1416, 1417, 1420)*

(2) any reference to the education of handicapped children and the education of all handicapped children and the provision of free public education to all handicapped children shall be deemed to be a reference to the provision of services to handicapped infants and toddlers in accordance with this part, and

(3) any reference to local educational agencies and intermediate educational agencies shall be deemed to be a reference to local service providers under this part.

ALLOCATION OF FUNDS

SEC. 684. (a) From the sums appropriated to carry out this part for any fiscal year, the Secretary may reserve 1 percent for payments to Guam, American Samoa, the Virgin Islands, the Republic of the Marshall Islands, the Federated State of Micronesia, the Republic of Palau, and the Commonwealth of the Northern Mariana Islands in accordance with their respective needs. *(20 USC 1484)*

(b)(1) The Secretary shall make payments to the Secretary of the Interior according to the need for such assistance for the provision of early intervention services to handicapped infants and toddlers and their families on reservations serviced by the elementary and secondary schools operated for Indians by the Department of the Interior. The amount of such payment for any fiscal year shall be 1.25 percent of the aggregate of the amount available to all States under this part for that fiscal year. *(20 USC 1484)*

(2) The Secretary of the Interior may receive an allotment under paragraph (1) only after submitting to the Secretary an application which meets the requirements of section 678 and which is approved by the Secretary. Section 616 shall apply to any such applications. *(20 USC 1416)*

(c)(1) For each of the fiscal years 1987 through 1991 from the funds remaining after the reservation and payments under subsections (a) and (b), the Secretary shall allot to each State an amount which bears the same ratio to the amount of such remainder as the number of infants and toddlers in the State bears to the number of infants and toddlers in all States, except that no State shall receive less than 0.15 percent of such remainder.

(2) For the purpose of paragraph (1)—

(A) the terms "infants" and "toddlers" mean children from birth to age 2, inclusive, and
(B) the term "State" does not include the jurisdictions described in subsection (a).
(d) If any State elects not to receive its allotment under subsection (c)(1), the Secretary shall reallot, among the remaining States, amounts from such State in accordance with such subsection.

AUTHORIZATION OF APPROPRIATIONS

SEC. 685. There are authorized to be appropriated to carry out this part $50,000,000 for fiscal year 1987, $75,000,000 for fiscal year 1988, and such sums as may be necessary for each of the 3 succeeding fiscal years. *(20 USC 1485)*

(b) STUDY OF SERVICES; COORDINATION OF ACTIONS. — (1) The Secretary of Education and the Secretary of Health and Human Services shall conduct a joint study of Federal funding sources and services for early intervention programs currently available and shall jointly act to facilitate interagency coordination of Federal resources for such programs and to ensure that funding available to handicapped infants, toddlers, children, and youth from Federal programs, other than programs under the Education of the Handicapped Act, is not being withdrawn or reduced. *(20 USC 1485 note)*

(2) Not later than 18 months after the date of the enactment of this Act, the Secretary of Education and the Secretary of Health and Human Services shall submit a joint report to the Congress describing the findings of the study conducted under paragraph (1) and describing the joint action taken under that paragraph. *(20 USC 1400)*

DATE DUE